BELIEVE GOD LOVES YOU

I find this a helpful, well-thought-out study guide. It brings strength and a broad span to scriptural study to deepen one's faith and provide a superb format for group dialogue and discussion. The author effectively lays out his faith journey and conviction.

Dennis Y. Ginoza, D.Min. Pastor
Fallbrook United Methodist Church

BELIEVE GOD LOVES YOU

His New Testament Promises

Marlin L Clark

Marlin Clark Publishing
Tustin, CA

Believe God Loves You
Bible study workbook edition.

Published in Tustin, California, by Marlin Clark Publishing

Unless otherwise noted, the Scripture quotations contained herein are from the New Revised Standard Version Bible, copyright © 1989, by the Division of Christian Education of the National Council of the Churches of Christ in the United States of America. Used by permission. All rights reserved.

Other Scripture references are from the following sources:

The Holy Bible, New International Version® (NIV), copyright © 1973, 1978, 1984 by the International Bible Society. All rights reserved throughout the world. Used by permission of International Bible Society.

The King James Version of the Bible (KJV).

Any underlining or bolding in the scripture quotations reflects the author's emphasis. Words in parentheses within a quote have been added by the author.

The poem "Preston," written by Delores Nitz, and an excerpt from the poem titled "Mama, Did You Know?" written by David L. Weatherford, are used with the authors' permission. Please visit www.davidlweatherford.com for more of David L. Weatherford's works. The Darrell Scott Testimony excerpt is a public record of the House Judiciary Committee. To the best of the publisher's knowledge, all other quoted stories are by unknown authors.

Clark, Marlin L
Believe God loves you / Marlin L Clark
ISBN: 978-0-9802495-3-8
1. Christian life. 2. Spirituality. 3. Religion. 4. Inspirational. I. Title.

Printed in the United States of America on acid-free paper
2 3 4 5 6 7 – 26 25 24 23 22 21

Dedication

To my father, LeRoy Clark, who journeyed in spirit on April 10, 2006, and my mother, Rebecca Clark, who journeyed in spirit on March 5, 2005. Although they did not seem to me to be my spiritual mentors during their lifetimes, it turns out that God was using them in my life in ways that I did not know, let alone understand. It was not until the final days of my Father's life that I began to realize how much God had influenced their lives and how much He had used their lives to influence my knowledge and understanding of Him.

Marlin L Clark

Table of Contents

CONTENTS

CONTENTS

Foreword

This book is about the Promises of God, which are available because of His incarnation as Jesus Christ. It is intended to help adult Christians of all levels of devotion find those things in their life that will bring them to a closer walk with God and allow them to claim more of His promises in their life. *Believe's* approach is unique in how <u>God's love</u> and what it means to <u>believe in Christ</u> are demonstrated through each of these promises. Each chapter illuminates one of the 14 promises using one key scripture and several supporting scriptures. Analysis, current examples, and personal experiences relate the scriptures to each of the promises.

Scripture, when directly quoted, is from one of three different translations. Most of the quotations are from the New Revised Standard Version; the following letter codes identify quotations from the other two versions.

KJV .... The King James Version
NIV .... The New International Version

Direct quotes from any standard translation are always italicized. Instances of either underlining or bold print indicate an emphasis added by the author. Words enclosed in parentheses within a quotation are descriptive words added by the author. Where the scriptures are paraphrased, they are not italicized.

Selecting which of the three translations to use on any particular scripture was based on which version most clearly presents the message related to the promise being illuminated. Those scriptures quoted from the KJV usually are ones that Marlin originally memorized from a King James Bible and do not sound right in any other translation.

The readers are encouraged to read the scriptures referenced in the reading lists from different translations and to read commentaries on those passages in conjunction with this study. Doing this will enhance your understanding of these Bible passages and help you to accept God's promises.

Believe illuminates those scriptures that have spoken to Marlin L Clark about each of these promises and provides commentary and personal examples on how he has related to God through these promises. Readers are encouraged to find additional scriptures and formulate their ideas on how they relate to God through each of these promises.

Acknowledgments

An endeavor that lasts as long as it has taken me to write this book is bound to involve several other persons. First, the members of a bible study group were the guinea pigs for the material. The ideas were more thoroughly developed, and grammar corrected as I presented each promise, the scriptures read, and thoughts and interpretations discussed. The vast difference between the original lessons and the current chapters is testimony to their significant effect.

Secondly, the adult Sunday school class members in Chappell, Nebraska, were the first to use the material without the benefit, or interference, of my interpretation. They also provided many helpful comments and corrections and additional scriptures they identified as appropriate for some of the promises.

Lastly, a trusted friend, Sy Tucker, was the first to read the material formatted as a book and to read it as an editor. Once these corrections were all incorporated, Yvonne Clark, my wife, performed a final read.

In addition to the persons involved in the first publication, others contributed to improved readability and clarity of thought in this revision. Lucinda Johnson, my daughter, is used to reading and editing my writing as we worked together for many years, and she frequently performed this function. As in times past, her thoughtful inputs have resulted in many improvements to this book. The second editor, David Johnson, my grandson, was the editor of his

ACKNOWLEDGEMENTS

college newspaper for two years and helped clarify some more philosophical points. Finally, Michelle Clark, my daughter-in-law, provided one more critical read after incorporating the corrections from the first two. As you can see, my family is an essential part of my life and continues to be one way God uses to improve my understanding of Him.

–Marlin L Clark

Introduction

The desire for the power of God's gifts in our lives is inherent within each Christian. How and to what degree we receive these gifts and how we use them in our lives is different for each believer. Although the Bible contains all the truth we need to receive and appropriately use these gifts, there does not seem to be any simple checklist that if we do these things, we will receive gift number one, another list for gift number two, etc. We seem to be trapped somewhere between what Christ told us about the simplicity necessary to know God: "*whoever does not receive the kingdom of God as a little child will never enter it*" (Luke 18:17b); and what Paul told the Roman Christians: "*there is no one who understands, no one who seeks God*" (Rom 3:11, NIV). *Believe* is firmly based on scripture, but not as a textbook. A Layperson wrote it in language that will bring these promises alive for today's Christians.

Believe God Loves You illuminates fourteen of the gifts that God has promised to all who believe in Jesus Christ and relates these gifts to the message of God's unlimited and unconditional love for each one of us. Each chapter discusses those scripture verses that identify each of the promises in the context of the larger body of scripture surrounding the specific verses quoted. The reader is encouraged to use the reading lists on the page opposite the first page of each chapter to enhance these scriptures' understanding. The reading lists include most

1

of the scriptures quoted in *Believe* plus additional verses before and after the quoted verses so that the reader will get a better sense of the quotes' context. For either group or individual study, reading the scriptures from the reading lists for the chapter at the start of each study period will help the reader(s) to understand the topics discussed in that chapter. There is space to write additional Scripture verses that each reader may feel are pertinent to each chapter's topic.

Each chapter ends with discussion questions and a call to action to help the reader claim each of God's Gifts in their own lives. Space is provided after each question for the reader to write their thoughts about that question. For group study, the questions provide a starting point for discussing the material after the leader has completed their presentation. Individuals can use the questions as a review of each chapter. The assignments should be completed between study sessions. In a group study, they provide an opening discussion for the next session. The questions and the call to action are located on the two pages following the end of each chapter.

Appendix B contains an evaluation form. Please complete this and either E-mail or snail mail it back to us. Your comments on the study are constructive.

You may also send us your comments by visiting our website, http://www.MarlinLClark.com, and using our guest book. The website also includes an electronic copy of the evaluation form that you can print or copy into an e-mail.

Reading List, God Loves You:

John 3:1-21   Matthew 6:1-34

Additional Scripture references:

_____

_____

Chapter 1, God Loves You

The words of the first promise are Christ's own words, as recorded in the third chapter of John.

For God so loved the world that he gave his only begotten son, that whosoever believed in him might not perish but have everlasting life (John 3:16, KJV).

John 3:16 is the basis for the New Testament. In many ways, this is what the rest of the New Testament is trying to get us to understand - the unlimited and unconditional love of God and His intent that we have everlasting life with Him. The loving relationship stated in this scripture is so different from what people have experienced with each other that even the incarnation of God, in the human body of Jesus Christ, and the real suffering that He endured as Christ, has not convinced very many of God's children to accept His promises. This chapter introduces the idea that each of God's promises is another way of our being able to understand and accept His love for us. As with all the other chapters, this chapter will show what we must do to respond to God and receive His Gifts.

You Must Be Born Again

If we look at the rest of the third chapter of John, we find that Jesus is in Jerusalem for the Passover feast, and He is telling Nicodemus that if he is to receive everlasting life with God that he must be "born again."

> *Very truly I tell you, no one can see the kingdom of God without being born from above* (John 3:3b).

Like Nicodemus, we do not understand what Christ is saying when He tells us that we must be "be born again" or "be born from above." From verse 16, we can conclude that what Christ means by being born from above is to "believe in Him." Most would accept that we are born again, of the Spirit, and from above when we truly accept and believe in Christ. The point where we may differ is the method or procedure by which this acceptance and belief in Christ occur. Some have experienced the change in an instant, like Paul on the road to Damascus. It is a lifetime process for others—that the belief and acceptance of God and Christ grow over time—with no specific time or event that marks the point of having accepted God. Still, others, like John Wesley, followed a lifelong process of searching and believing. However, there was a specific point when the assurance of the rebirth was complete. As Wesley put it, "my heart was strangely warmed." There are also those who may not publicly declare their acceptance of Christ, but the fact that they have accepted is discernable by how they live their lives.

Our Concern Is; Knowing That We Have Accepted Christ

As individual Christians, we need to remember that <u>it is not our concern </u>how someone else has accepted Christ. <u>Our concern is knowing that we have accepted Christ</u>. Acceptance of faith is a personal journey. We each are responsible for our acceptance of Christ, and then we can claim His promises. Only then can we truly accept His gift of the Son as the complete and final sacrifice for our sins. And we can begin to understand how His unconditional love can change our lives.

Regardless of how you come to understand the mark of acceptance of God the Father, Christ the Son, and the Holy Spirit — each of us must accept Christ and be born again before we can receive any of His promises. Understanding and acceptance are also necessary before we can incorporate His unconditional love into our own lives.

Christ Not Sent to Judge

For God sent not his Son into the world to condemn the world; but that the world through him might be saved (John 3:17, KJV).

In the next verse, John 3:17, Christ tells us that God did not send Christ to judge us but to save us. First, verse 16 tells us God is willing – through His incarnation as Christ – to suffer all our sins so that we might live with Him everlastingly. Second, verse 17 tells us that Christ is not interested in judging us but in saving us. However, the two verses come as a pair. We must accept the sacrifice of Christ for ourselves – "believe in Him" – before we can receive the gift of everlasting life with God. If we do not accept Christ and His sacrifice, we have left ourselves under God's judgment because of our sin of not believing. We separate ourselves from the promises of God in the New Testament if we do not accept Christ as our personal savior. There will be no Holy Spirit in our lives to guide our thoughts and actions or provide His power in our lives. Also, there is no one to intercede for us with God the Father if we do not accept Christ. To accept all of God's promises, we must believe in Christ as our personal savior and have our priorities straight relative to how we live our lives. Of course, the primary reason for knowing God and accepting Christ as our personal savior is that we want to spend eternity with Him. However, eternity starts now, and when we accept God's love in our lives, it is a great power to help us live our lives today. There are events in our lives that would be unbearable without the acceptance of Christ and the presence of the Holy Spirit. The following poem provides an example of how God can and does work in our lives today.

—☼—

Preston

"He's deaf - He cannot hear,"
The words filled my heart with fear;
As I rocked him and held him near,
This tiny baby I love so dear.
I rocked and talked - -even sang a song,
And often wondered what could have gone wrong.
I held him close and prayed every day
Asking the Lord to take the deafness away.
Then deep in my heart, the Lord planted a thought,
"If he never hears your voice it matters not,
My Spirit will lead him to make the right choice
And in his spirit he'll hear my voice."
Then I prayed -- Oh Lord, help me to be
In tune with your plans so that he
Can have every opportunity to learn of Thee,
This lovely grandson you've given to me.
Love him, guide him, show him the way,
Entrusting us to help each day.
Give us the knowledge that can only come from you,
Then whatever the problems, we'll make it through

Delores Nitz, 11-17-1989

—☼—

As you might be able to discern, this poem is from the pen of a loving and born-again Christian grandmother after she discovered that her new grandson was deaf. As you read the poem, you can see the process of God's love taking over this

8

grandmother's fear; of a child being born without all of the senses we expect. The emotions expressed by Delores Nitz in this poem show an acceptance of the promise of God's love in her life. The words show us how this acceptance of God has changed her outlook on all of life. If you reread the poem, you will see another aspect of this grandmother's life. She has focused her energy on God. In addition to being aware of the message in John 3:16-17, she is also mindful of Christ's message in Matthew 6:33.

God Must Be First

> *But seek ye first the kingdom of God, and his righteousness; and all these things shall be added unto you* (Matt. 6:33, KJV).

John 3:16 tells us of God's infinite and unconditional love, but in the sixth chapter of Matthew, Christ reminds us that there are things that we do in our lives that can keep us from being able to accept that unlimited and unconditional love. What Christ tells us we need to do is simple, right? All we have to do to allow God's love to operate in our lives and to be able to recognize and accept all of God's promises is to put Him first! Well, it is simple, but it is not easy. As previously stated, it is all about our priorities! What is first in your life: your family, church, success, job, personal enjoyment, or God? How you might answer this question verbally and in the context of reading a book about God's gifts may not agree with how you answer the question each day with your actions. The honest answer is the same as the answer to the question: how do you spend most of your time each day. Does God come first only on Sunday? Or maybe not even on Sunday! How much time do you spend watching, participating in, or thinking about sporting events compared to the time you spend praying to, thinking about, listening to, and worshiping God? Does "Super Bowl Sunday" sound like something that puts God first?

How much time do you spend in prayer each day? How much time do you spend reading the Bible each day? How much time do you spend reading Spiritual material each day? How much time do you spend doing God's work each day? How much time do you spend thanking God for the gift of His Son each day? Moreover, how much time do you spend thanking God for what He is doing in your life? Let us look again at the keywords in Christ's discussion about our priorities.

> *But seek ye first the kingdom of God, and his righteousness; and all these things will be added unto you* (Matt. 6:33, KJV).

Well, what does this mean to me today? Let us look at the context of this one verse of scripture as a part of the entire chapter. The sixth chapter of Matthew is talking about:

vv. 1-4: Give in Secret.

vv. 5-6: Pray in Secret.

vv. 7-15: Our model for praying is the Lord's Prayer.

vv. 16-18: Fast in Secret;

vv. 19-21: True treasures are not stored on earth but in heaven.

vv. 22-23: Your eye must be clear, or your body will be filled with darkness.

v. 24: You cannot be a slave to possessions and give your life to God. And finally,

vv. 25-34: Put Your Trust in God!

Do not worry about your day-to-day physical needs! These needs are *"the other things"* that Christ is talking about in Matthew 6:33.

Put Aside Human Priorities

We understand the gift of God's love is unconditional, and we believe that Christ died for our sins, but if we want to see the results of God's love in our lives, if we're going to claim the promise of John 3:16, then we must put God first in our lives. We must put aside our human priorities and accept God's priorities in our lives. We must spend the majority of our time each day searching for God, conversing with God, studying about God, listening to God, thanking God, and acting on what God tells us! We not only need to believe John 3:16, but we also need to rely on it every day. Our actions need to demonstrate that reliance. And no, requiring action on our part does not make God's love conditional. Our activity is necessary so that we can accept God's love that is unconditionally given.

Now you might say I do not have time for all of that each day. I have a family to take care of; I need a job to pay the rent so that my family will have a roof over their head. Surely, God does not want me to neglect my duties toward my family. After all, didn't God ordain marriage and family? Anyhow, I am a lot more comfortable with the idea of God's unconditional love than I am thinking that I actually may need to change my life to accept His "unconditional" love. Anyway, I pray each evening and usually say grace before my meals. Moreover, I typically go to church on Sunday. I do not have any more time in the week to spend reading the Bible.

Well, let us go back to the scripture, Christ's words, and see just what parts we did not understand.

Seek ye first – that is not very ambiguous. This phrase is not subject to different interpretations. First does not have very many meanings regardless of how you use it. If anything is first, that always means there is nothing that comes before it. This concept is not new, and it was not new in the time of Christ. It is straight from the Ten Commandments. "*Thou shalt have no other gods before me.*" (Exod. 20:3, KJV).

The Key Word is GOD

The Kingdom of God – now we could all come up with different specific definitions for the kingdom of God. We might also argue about exactly where it is, whether it is now or when it will come, but that would just be using our words to avoid what we know is the keyword, God! The key word in the phrase is not kingdom; the keyword is GOD.

God must be first in our lives, every day, all of every day, for the rest of our lives. Not because God's love is conditional, it is not. The problem is our free will. We are free to ignore God and the promise of John 3:16. If we are to receive the benefits of God's love, we must consciously choose to put God first in our lives. It is that simple. That is our part of the bargain.

And what is God's part, other than salvation? We do not have to sweat the small stuff! His love for us, as demonstrated by the sacrifice of Jesus Christ, is ours to claim. All of His promises are ours to claim. To paraphrase what it says in Matthew 6:25. I am telling you not to worry about your life and what you are to eat, or about your body, and what you are to wear. We do not have to worry about our daily needs, not any of them. The Bible says, "All of these things." However, there is a downside to this. If we continue to worry about our physical needs, we demonstrate that we either do not believe what God promises in the Bible, or we do not trust Him to fulfill those promises. Is there a question in your mind as to whether God is God? On the other hand, is there a question as to whether Christ is His Son and whether His death was the complete and final sacrifice for all the world's sins?

Before any of you decide that, I am saying you should just tear up all your bills and sit and wait for God to send Ed McMahan with a $10,000,000 check. Or that you should wait for the lottery to pick your number when the jackpot is over $100,000,000. Let us look one more time at some of the other words in the sixth chapter of Matthew. In verse 34, it uses the word worry; it says, do not *worry* about tomorrow. The verse does not say sit and do nothing; it says; do not worry.

God Will Direct You

Trust that God will direct you in a way that will solve tomorrow's problems. Seek ye first does not say that you do nothing but pray all day, every day. It says that searching for, communicating with, thanking, and acting on the things God reveals to you must be the essential part of your life. It says that you need to consult God about your life decisions, listen for His guidance, and then actually follow it.

I will promise you that if you truly accept what the scripture tells us in John 3:16 and follow God's directions and His plan for your life, you will not spend much time being idle. You will find that doing God's work and seeking His kingdom are not mutually exclusive activities. You actually can be seeking the kingdom of God while you are doing His work. Fortunately, everything that you do within His direction is His work. Let me say that again.

Everything that you do within His direction is His work.

You can be sure that God expects you to make the best use of the talents that He has given you. Until you ask and receive an answer, you cannot be sure that how you are using those talents today is what His plan is for you.

What if I have not been putting God first in my life, and I do not know what His plan is for me? Maybe I am not very sure about His unconditional love. Perhaps it is still a little hard to understand what God has done and is doing for me. Do I believe that God loved me so much that He sacrificed His son to redeem me? The answers to these questions are available through your PRAYER and PATIENCE. These words must be your guide for each day if you want to live your life to the fullest and claim the promises that God has made to you through Christ.

Keep a Daily Journal

Keep a journal of your day with God. What are the things that you did today that brought you closer to God? Were there any things that you did today that tended to separate you from God? Do you feel like God's love is working through you? Spend a few moments to write down your thoughts about why you think God's love either is or is not working through you.

Are you working on your prayer life? Are you working on being patient, waiting for His answers? Do you want to know what to pray, how to pray, and the conditions or requirements God places upon you? These are the topics for Chapter 2.

Discussion:

1. What does being born again mean to you? _____

   _____

   a. Has the study of Chapter 3 of John changed your understanding or belief in any way? _____
      i. If it has, what beliefs have the study changed, and how have they been changed? _____

         _____

         _____

2. Do you believe that you have been "born again?" _____
   a. If so, how did it happen to you? _____

      _____

   b. If not, explain how you think it should happen in your life. _____

      _____

3. Is God first in your life? _____
   a. List Each day's significant activities for one week; put an * by each of the activities that involve God in your life. _____

      _____

   b. Do the activities with asterisks account for more time than those without asterisks? _____
      i. If they do not, what do you need to do to fix your priorities? _____

         _____

         _____

Call to Action:

1. Keep a journal of your day with God. The journal needs to be in a separate notebook, in your PDA, or on your computer. The following suggestions are the minimum entries you should make for each day.

    a. What did you do today that brought you closer to God?

    b. What did you do today that tended to separate you from God?

    c. What changes do you intend to make to adjust your priorities to what God wants in your life?

Reading List, Prayer:

Romans 8:18-30	Matthew 6:1-15
Luke 11:1-4	Matthew 7:7-11
John 15:1-17	1 John 4:7-21

Additional Scripture references:

_____

_____

Chapter 2, Prayer

If we accept and believe in God, then it follows that we would be interested in expanding our knowledge of God and finding what His plans are for us. Wanting to know His plans lead us to the topic of prayer, the second promise, and our second opportunity to examine God's love for each of us. We will also investigate what it means to believe in Him.

The promise about prayer is from Romans. Paul is speaking about a Christian's spiritual life. He tells us that if we do not know how to pray, the Holy Spirit will help us.

> *Likewise the Spirit helps us in our weakness; for we do not know how to pray as we ought, but that very Spirit intercedes with sighs too deep for words. And God, who searches the heart, knows what is the mind of the Spirit, because the Spirit intercedes for the saints according to the will of God* (Rom. 8:26-27).

The New Jerusalem translation uses "the holy people" rather than "the saints" to identify for whom the Spirit will intercede. I think that is better as it seems more inclusive. We can all try to be "holy people," but few of us will ever think of ourselves as "saints." Regardless of how we view ourselves today, if we want to understand and accept God's promises, we must learn to communicate with Him! We need to ask God to give us that which He has promised. We need to ask God to replace the free will that He gave us with His will. In other words, we must pray.

Excuses

To many, the idea of talking with God is frightening. We hear statements like: I do not know how to pray; I do not know what to pray for; God does not seem to answer my prayers; I cannot pray in front of others; I am not comfortable praying, or my mind wanders when I pray. These are all excuses I have used to explain why I did not pray or not Pray very often. The New Testament asks and answers all of these perceived problems. If we look again at the scripture above, Paul has already told us that "*we do not know how to pray as we ought,*" so we should not feel like we are alone if we do not know how to pray or are uncomfortable in prayer. To help us be more comfortable in prayer by letting the Holy Spirit help us, let us turn to the scriptures to answer each of these excuses.

How Should I Pray

I do not know how to pray. – According to the sixth chapter of Matthew, Christ had been talking about praying. He told the disciples not to pray like the pagans, babbling, thinking that their gods will hear them because of the number of words they use. Christ then told the disciples:

> *"This, then, is how you should pray: 'Our Father in heaven, hallowed be your name, your kingdom come, your will be done on earth as it is in heaven. Give us today our daily bread. Forgive us our debts, as we also have forgiven our debtors. And lead us not into temptation, but deliver us from the evil one.' For if you forgive men when they sin against you, your heavenly Father will also forgive you. But if you do not forgive men their sins, your Father will not forgive your sins'"* (Matt 6:9-15, NIV).

We have memorized and use the words we know as "The Lord's Prayer" as a specific prayer for many occasions. Most Christian churches will use it as a congregational prayer sometime in each service. However, if we look at the context of Christ's statement, "This then is how you should pray," He had been talking about how the Jewish hypocrites and the pagans prayed. The hypocrites prayed for show, and the pagans used all the words they could to try to get their god's attention. Christ was giving the disciples a model of what a sincere prayer should be. He was not telling the disciples that these specific words were the only words to use when we pray. Christ prayed about everything, and He prayed for extended periods. From this, we can conclude that Christ was telling the disciples, and through the Bible is telling us today, the elements of the Lord's Prayer are the elements that we need to include in our prayers. Christ did not say this is *what* you should pray; He said this is *how* you should pray: First, we need to acknowledge the Lord as our creator, not profane His name, and declare our desire for His kingdom. Second, we ask for the things we need - the essential things of life - food for each day. Last but of equal importance, we are to ask for forgiveness. We have all sinned, and we all need forgiveness. In the Lord's Prayer, we are reminded that for us to be forgiven, we must forgive everyone who has sinned against us! It is not that God's forgiveness is conditional. We cannot accept God's forgiveness for our sins if we have not forgiven others of their sins against us.

Our Model for Prayer

If we accept that the Lord's Prayer should be the model for our prayers, how do we apply it? One way to acknowledge God and His majesty is to start by thanking Him for His creation. Thank Him for this day that He has given you, and for whatever it is you are most grateful for today - maybe even for the problems that He has given you. Reflect on how events in your life help you to grow and provide opportunities for knowing Him better. Continuing this thankful attitude throughout a prayer helps us keep our desire for God's kingdom foremost in our thoughts as we pray. We can declare our passion for His kingdom by continually seeking His will relative to each of our requests. As we ask for forgiveness from God, He will remind us of those we need to forgive. If we listen carefully, He will even give us actions. Following what God tells you to do is another way to declare your desire for His kingdom.

Although we teach our children to say the Lord's Prayer, it is not a children's prayer. The real meaning is beyond most children. According to the eleventh chapter of Luke's gospel, Christ gave this prayer to the disciples when one of them asked Him to teach them to pray. The words recorded there, essentially what we now call the Lord's Prayer, were for the disciples. Only on the lips of a disciple does the prayer have its full meaning. Assuming that we are all trying to be disciples, the Lord's Prayer is the model or formula we should use to construct our prayers. This is not to say that God requires a specific formula for a prayer to be acceptable. He only requires us to be honest and sincere. It is to say that using the Lord's Prayer as a model will gradually help us express our thoughts better to God - which will result in helping us to be more open to God's plan for us. Following the Lord's Prayer structure will also help keep us from attempting to bend the will of God to our desires rather than submitting our will to the will of God.

What Should I Pray For?

I do not know what to pray for. – The Bible answers this problem in several places. In the Lord's Prayer, Christ tells us to ask for our daily bread, which tells us that God is interested in all our needs, even the most mundane. For some reason, we tend to think that we have to filter our thoughts and requests from what we want to what we believe will interest God and not offend God. On the contrary, the Bible tells us that God already knows our thoughts. So why do we think that it will work to try to filter them in our prayers? All we are doing is telling God that we believe we can hide things from Him. Which essentially is saying that we do not think that God is God! The Bible also tells us:

> *Ask and it will be given to you*
> (Matt. 7:7a, NIV).

This scripture certainly does not imply any limitations on which thoughts, requests, or desires should be included in our prayers. Also:

> *If you abide in me, and my words abide in you, ask for whatever you wish, and it will be done for you* (John 15:7).

Prayer is part of our learning process from God. When we pray about everything in our lives and pray for all of our desires, God can correct our thoughts and desires by how He answers our prayers. He will make us aware of the things in our lives that keep us from "abiding in Him." When we act on God's directions, we have already started to work on the answer to our next excuse.

Where are His Answers?

God does not seem to answer my prayers. – This is one of the more difficult problems to resolve in our communication with God. Prayer sometimes appears to be our monologue rather than a dialogue with God. Our communication with God generally is not the same as a dialogue with another person. We do not usually get short-term feedback that acknowledges God is listening and understands. At least in my case, I do not hear a clear verbal response with the answers to my questions in the sequence they were asked. When we also consider that God often does not give us the solution we want or the timing we expect - as stated in the section above - we may not be "abiding

23

in Him." It is not surprising that we may feel God is not answering our prayers.

This perception can severely limit our relationship with God if we do not come to understand what we must do to receive and understand God's answers to our prayers. As mentioned in Appendix C, Authors Testimony, I have had a recent experience with specific answers to prayer. The timing was not mine, and the answers were not what I expected; they were much better.

God's Answers are Better than Our Expectations

I had been praying for several years that God would show me how and when to approach my father regarding the fact that he was never baptized. Also, as far as I knew, he had never accepted Christ. I had prayed for both Mom and Dad to journey in spirit together as Mom was in a lot of pain, and with the mental loss from over 20 years of Parkinson's disease, we were sure that Dad would be lost without Mom. The movie ending to "The Notebook" would have fit my request perfectly. My parents were married for over 78 years, and both were ready to go. Throughout their marriage, they always helped each other with any problems. Each was holding on so that they would not leave the other one alone. As far as I knew, God had not answered any of my prayers relative to my parents. When Mom died in March of 2005, we thought Dad might just quit eating and follow pretty soon, but that did not happen. I questioned God as to why Dad was still around. Dad frequently stated that he no longer was of any value to himself or anyone else and was very lonesome.

A little over a year after Mom died, on April 10, 2006, my father journeyed in Spirit at the age of ninety-nine. I spent eight nights, including the night he died, sitting with my father after he broke a hip and had surgery to fix it. For a long time, I felt there was something that I needed to do to bring my dad to Christ. As I have always idealized my dad, this was a complicated task to ponder, let alone perform. I had often prayed that God would give me the opportunity and inspiration to approach this with my father. After my mother, at the age of 100, died on March 5, 2005, Dad frequently stated, "Mom was calling him." On reflection, this was the first time my sister or I could remember him even acknowledging there was an afterlife—Progress, but not the answer I wanted.

God Directs Us to His Answers

I began to feel that I had missed an opportunity that God had given me. My Bible study friends counseled me to give the problem to God. I did intellectually, but not totally. I still worried and prayed for Dad's salvation. During those evenings I spent with him in the hospital, God started pointing me to scriptures that indicated that I should no longer worry. This direction from God was especially true after it became evident that Dad no longer wanted to live as he refused to eat or drink anything. The first scripture that God brought to my attention was 1 John 4:16. This scripture is not a scripture that I remembered reading before. Probably because what it says did not speak to me any of the previous times I read it. Two nights after his surgery, as I was sitting with Dad in the hospital, this scripture came to my attention through a book I was reading. I went down to the chapel in the hospital to read the entire fourth chapter and found the answer to one of my prayers relative to Dad. The scripture told me:

> *God is love, and those who abide in love abide*
> *in God, and God abides in them* (1 John 4:16b).

In general, I would not take just a part of a verse of scripture as a total message, and as I said, I read the entire fourth chapter that night. However, because I know God himself directed me to the specific verse quoted above, I knew God was using this scripture to show me I did not need to worry about His relationship with Dad. God was telling me that even though, as far as I knew, Dad had never publicly declared his acceptance of Christ, their relationship was all right. Dad lived his life witnessing his love for his family and his love and respect for others. Further, since God is the source of love, this verse, which God had told me to read, said I should not be concerned about HIS relationship with Dad.

The Harvest Belongs to God

Christ charged us with spreading the Good News, but we are not responsible for the harvest. Dad certainly knew what I believed, and now God was telling me through the scriptures that the harvest was at least in progress, if not complete.

The second verse that God pointed me to during these eight days was:

And we know that all things work together for good to them that love God, to them who are the called according to his purpose (Rom. 8:28, KJV).

The thought came to me the night Dad died. He had claimed this promise several times in his life. The loss of his right arm at the shoulder when he was 11 was a tragedy and could have left him handicapped for life, but it did not. Dad did not think that he was handicapped, and I do not know anyone who knew him and worked with him that ever thought that either. He was a stronger person in the end than he would have been, having not had that accident. If Dad was able to claim this promise, in his way, in a way that was acceptable to God, he must have known and loved the Lord. Dad certainly lived his life as if he loved the righteousness of the Lord. There was at least one reason that Dad lived for a little over a year after Mom died. Through God, he was still teaching me lessons about life. If we listen and wait for God's timing, He will answer our prayers! Believe those answers will be better than we ever could have imagined.

Why Should I Pray in Public?

I cannot pray in front of others – There are words in the Bible that tell us that we should not pray in public! For example, Matthew quotes Christ as saying:

> *But when you pray, go into your room, close the door and pray to your Father, who is unseen. Then your Father, who sees what is done in secret, will reward you* (Matt. 6:6, NIV).

This scripture is telling us two things. First, our prayers are about *our* relationship with God. We do not need anyone else present to enable them; they are our petition to God. Second, we are not supposed to be trying to impress anyone else. God knows our needs regardless of the words we use. Prayer is necessary for us to express our needs to God and submit our will to His will. Praying as part of a group can be a profoundly spiritual experience where all share common concerns and are looking to submit their choices to God's will. If it bothers you to pray in front of others, you are praying to the wrong audience. Remember, you are praying to God!

Similarly, if you compare your prayers to others or judge other's prayers to be "somewhat lacking in their presentation," you do not recognize God's love and respect for everyone. Prayer must be a regular part of your life, in private or with other believers, wherever you are and in all situations. If you have problems praying with others, suggest that each person offer a sentence prayer. Practicing with a sentence prayer can help you learn to be open to God in the presence of others.

Prayer is Not Comfortable for Me

I am not comfortable praying – Praying is something like any learning process. You will never be comfortable praying if you never start praying. Saying that you are uncomfortable implies that you do not think your prayers are good enough and that someone may criticize how you pray. Worrying about being comfortable absolutely misses the point of prayer. We are not praying for other people's approval, and we are not even praying for approval by God. We pray because we need to worship God and acknowledge our dependence upon God. If we are not comfortable with prayer, we either do not understand the point of prayer or are uncomfortable with God. If the latter is true, then we need to go back and look at John 3:17 again.

> *For God sent not his Son into the world to condemn the world; but that the world through him might be saved* (John 3:17, KJV).

No matter what we have done, if we go to God in prayer, confessing our sins and looking for God's help to "sin no more," our relationship with God should be one of being comforted rather than causing us to be uncomfortable. Prayer, if practiced frequently, will become one of the most comforting activities of our lives.

My Mind Wanders

My mind wanders when I pray – How do you know that the thoughts coming into your mind are not God responding to your prayer? We need to listen to those wanderings of the mind, as they might be God responding to us. However, we also need to verify any responses we think we have received from God to ensure they are consistent with the Bible and common sense. Not all responses we receive while we are praying are from God! The Bible tells us that the tempter may come to us through our innermost thoughts and desires. He launches his attack in our minds.

A level of discipline in your prayer time can help if your wanderings are just distractions. Before you start, make a list of what and for whom you need to pray. Praying aloud may also help focus your mind on your praise of God; and then on your petitions to God. If while you are quiet and waiting for God to speak to you, your mind still wanders, talk to God about the distractions. Let Him help you focus your thought process. If you still are not sure about your prayer life, the following story about prayer may give you some inspiration.

The Weight of Our Prayers

A poorly dressed woman with a look of defeat on her face walked into a grocery store. She approached the store owner in a most humble manner and asked if he would let her charge a few groceries. She softly explained that her husband was very ill and unable to work; they had seven children and needed food. The grocer scoffed at her and requested that she leave his store.

Visualizing the family needs, she said, "Please, sir! I will bring you the money just as soon as I can." He told her he could not give her credit as she did not have a charge account at his store.

Standing beside the counter was a customer who overheard the conversation between the two. The customer walked forward and told the grocer that he would stand good for whatever she needed for her family.

The grocer said in a very reluctant voice, "Do you have a grocery list?" She replied, "Yes sir."

"O.K.," he said, "put your grocery list on the scales, and whatever your grocery list weighs, I will give you that amount in groceries." She hesitated a moment with a bowed head. Then, she reached into her purse, took out a piece of paper, and scribbled something on it. She then laid the piece of paper on the scale carefully with her head still bowed.

Both the grocer and the customer's eyes showed amazement as the scales went down and stayed down. The grocer, staring at the scales, turned slowly to the customer and said begrudgingly, "I can't believe it."

The customer smiled, and the grocer started putting the groceries on the other side of the scale. The scale did not balance, so he continued to put more and more groceries on them until the scales would hold no more.

The grocer stood there in utter disgust. Then, finally, he grabbed the piece of paper from the scales and looked at it with greater amazement. It was not a grocery list; it was a prayer, which said:

"Dear Lord, you know my needs, and I am leaving this in your hands."

The grocer gave her the groceries he had gathered and stood in stunned silence. The woman thanked him and left the store. The customer handed a fifty-dollar bill to the grocer and said, "It was worth every penny of it." Only God knows how much a prayer weighs.

We Must Pray

The bottom line is that we must pray. The most significant limitations to our feeling at one with God are: our not praying enough, not being completely open with God in acknowledging our every thought and need, and not being open to His responses to our prayers. Any time we are tempted not to pray, there are a few things we should remember.

1) We need all the help we can get to live this life to God's plan for us.

2) God is never too busy to listen; we should never be too busy to call on Him.

3) Practice makes perfect.

4) There is nothing too big or too small about which to pray.

5) We must be ever vigilant to verify the source of all responses we receive.

6) An effective prayer life must also include the active study of the Bible; and

    7) What God wants for each one of us is so much greater than we will ever imagine on our own that once we see His plan unfolding in our lives, we will never again want to be without His guidance.

Start a Prayer Journal

One of the most effective means of improving your prayer life can be to start a prayer journal. Including it as a part of your daily journal will spotlight the effect of prayer in discovering your relationship with God. Keep a running list of the petitions you have made to God; include dates and all of the circumstances that make this petition important to you. In the same journal, keep a list of those things you feel God has revealed to you, the date, the circumstances, and the method.

Look for Correlations

Periodically, you should look for correlations between the petitions and the revelations. You will be amazed at how many of your prayers God is answering and how God is working in your life to make your petitions more reflective of what He wants for you. You will also be surprised at how God's desires for your life are much better than the desires you have for yourself. Prayer will enhance your feeling of the presence of The Holy Spirit in your life, which is the subject of the next chapter.

Discussion:

1. Why do we need to pray? _____
   _____

2. Do you pray as often as you think you should? _____
   a. List the times or events in a typical day when you
      pray. _____
      _____
      _____

   b. List what you pray about. _____
      _____

3. Do you think that you would feel closer to God if you
   prayed more? _____

4. Look in your Bible concordance or an online search
   engine and find more scripture references about prayer.
   List each scripture and a few words about what it says
   to you about prayer. _____
   _____

5. Do you ever feel that your prayers are inadequate? ____
   a. Explain why if you answered yes. _____
      _____

6. Do you expect God to answer your prayers? _____
   a. Is there an event in your life that you recognized as
      an answer to a prayer? A prayer that God seemed to
      ignore for a long time? Note the event and a few
      words of how you know that this was an answer
      from God. _____
      _____
      _____

7. Do you ever feel that God does not answer your
   prayers? _____
   a. Explain why _____
      _____

8. List the things that you need to do to improve your
   prayer life. _____
   _____

Call to Action:

1. Make a separate section in your daily journal for your prayers.
   a. Number and date them as a running list of requests.
   b. Include the circumstances around the prayer request and anything that makes it unique.
2. Make a separate section in your daily journal for God's responses.
   a. Number and date them as a running list of responses.
   b. Include the circumstances around the response and anything that makes it unique.
   c. If an answer responds to a specific prayer, look back at the prayer request list and cross-reference the numbers. Also, note the correlations in your daily journal for that day.
3. Periodically review your prayer list and response list and look for correlations other than those that were obvious when the response was received. Cross-reference the numbers in each list.
   a. If there are areas of requests and responses that you are unsure about, note them in your daily journal and pray about the confusion.

Reading List, The Holy Spirit:

Luke 11:5-13   Acts 1:1-11
Matthew 3:1-17   John 15:1-8
John 20:19-23   John 14:22-31
Acts 2:1-47   Acts 4:23-31
Acts 8:9-25

Additional Scripture references:

_____

_____

Chapter 3, The Holy Spirit

The third promise is the Holy Spirit!

If you then, who are evil, know how to give good gifts to your children, how much more will the heavenly Father give the Holy Spirit to those who ask him. (Luke 11:13)

Christ promised the power of the Holy Spirit!

You will receive power when the Holy Spirit has come upon you; (Acts 1:8b).

Christ tells us in the gospel of Luke that the Holy Spirit is better and more important than any gift that we could bestow upon our children. Luke tells us in the book of Acts that the promise of the Holy Spirit is the promise of power in our lives! What more evidence of God's love for us could we ask when He provides for each one of us the ultimate power in the universe? What better way to show us His unlimited and unconditional love and what it means to "be born from above" than by giving us the power of the Holy Spirit!

The Holy Spirit Was Present at Creation

"In the beginning God (Elohim) created the heaven and the earth. And the earth was without form, and void; and darkness was upon the face of the deep. And the Spirit of God moved upon the face of the waters" (Gen 1:1-2, KJV).

35

In the Hebrew text, the word used for God is Elohim, which is plural, signifying the presence of the Trinity from the beginning—Elohim: Father, Son, and Holy Spirit. The second verse makes it more specific, *"...the Spirit of God moved upon the face of the waters."* The Spirit of God, or the Holy Spirit, has therefore been present for all of time.

Father, Son, and Holy Spirit

All three personalities of God: Father, Son, and Holy Spirit have existed since before time began and will continue to exist after the end of time. They are all eternal. In Catherine Marshall's book *"The Helper,"* she states that the Holy Spirit is a person and paraphrases Christ by saying that the Holy Spirit is God's contemporary expression. When the disciples talked to Christ about His leaving, He told them that He would not leave them as orphans. The Holy Spirit replaced the physical presence of Christ on this earth as God's presence within each one of us forever. The Holy Spirit's presence within each believer is significant because – while Christ was limited by being in a physical body, the Holy Spirit has no such limitations – therefore, Christ, as the Holy Spirit, is present within all believers at all times.

Filled With the Holy Spirit

Both the Old and New Testaments tell us that the Holy Spirit empowered specific persons for specific tasks. When the angel told Zechariah he would father a son and that this son, John, "would be filled with the Holy Spirit" from birth. Matthew and Luke tell us that the Holy Spirit descended upon Christ like a dove when John baptized Him. However, the Holy Spirit first became generally available to all believers at Pentecost.

And when Jesus had been baptized, just as he
came up from the water, suddenly the heavens were
opened to him and he saw the Spirit of God

descending like a dove and alighting on him. And a voice from heaven said, "This is my Son, the Beloved, with whom I am well pleased."
(Matt. 3:16-17).

Jesus' ministry started when He received the power of the Holy Spirit. Until we receive the Holy Spirit into our lives, we are constrained in what we can do. Without the Holy Spirit, we are limited to just our raw talents and capabilities. So Christ tells us in John:

because apart from me you can do nothing.
(John 15:5b).

You Can Command God's Power

Yes, there were special cases where individuals received the power of the Holy Spirit before Pentecost, but this must have been different because Christ told His disciples they would need to wait for a time after He ascended so that He could send "the Comforter." Christ said that he would not leave them alone even though he was returning to the Father. As "the Comforter," the Holy Spirit became available to all believers. When we receive the Holy Spirit, God's power not only works through us, but we can command that power. For instance, again in the book of John:

*Jesus said to them again, "Peace be with you. As the Father has sent me, so I send you." When he had said this, he breathed on them and said to them, "Receive the Holy Spirit. **If you forgive the sins of any, they are forgiven them; if you retain the sins of any, they are retained."***
(John 20:21-23).

Now that is POWER! Operating as an agent of God is the power that the Holy Spirit can bring to each of us if we accept it. The ability for the disciples to forgive or retain sins was a particular case before Pentecost. Before the time when God made the full power of the Holy Spirit available to all believers.

However, receiving the Holy Spirit carries an obligation. If we look at the rest of the verse in Acts quoted at the beginning of this chapter:

> *and you will be my witnesses in Jerusalem, in all Judea and Samaria, and to the ends of the earth* (Acts 1:8b).

We Must Witness

God expects us to use the Holy Spirit! A part of God's plan for each of us is to witness about our relationship with Him. The Bible states this without question. Now we must determine how we are to perform that witness. John 14:26 tells us that the Holy Spirit will teach us what we need to know to enable our witnessing to those around us about our relationship with God.

> *I have said these things to you while I am still with you. But the Advocate, the Holy Spirit, whom the Father will send in my name, will teach you everything, and remind you of all that I have said to you* (John 14:25-26).

The Holy Spirit not only empowers us; the Holy Spirit will also teach us everything we need to know about our witness.

If you still do not know how you witness about how God is working in your life, there are two possible explanations. Either you have not received the Holy Spirit, or you are not listening to what the Holy Spirit is directing you to do. Peter said in Acts:

> *Repent, and be baptized every one of you in the name of Jesus Christ so that your sins may be forgiven; and you will receive the gift of the Holy Spirit* (Acts 2:38).

Repent!

Repent and be baptized in the name of Jesus Christ. What a simple, straightforward command, but seemingly difficult for most of us. Note the sequence; first, you REPENT. Second, you are baptized. The baptism that Peter is talking about here has no meaning without repentance.

Moreover, after repentance, this is not your ordinary baptism by water. It is baptism "in the name of Jesus Christ." Another way of saying this is that we must die to our old nature so that Christ's nature may live within us. We are fearful of giving up control of our lives to God, of bearing our souls to God, of committing ourselves publicly to seek and follow God's will in our lives. We are afraid of accepting a baptism that is not just a symbol. Again, this is not a baptism with water. Most of us have had a water baptism either as an infant, child, or adult. However, we are afraid of baptism "in the name of Jesus Christ." We are scared of asking God, Christ, and the Holy Spirit to take over and control our lives.

Ask God

What is the source of this fear? It is either an incomplete understanding or a misunderstanding of what God wants with us and for us. There is no reason to be afraid of repenting. Do we believe that God is God? Then we cannot hide anything from Him. He knows our every thought. Our act of repentance is simply our acknowledgment of our transgressions and our declaring a willingness to accept responsibility for them so we can accept God's forgiveness and receive the Holy Spirit to empower and guide us. God does not force the Holy Spirit upon us, as this would violate our free will. Therefore, we must *ask* God to fill us with the Holy Spirit. We must *permit* Him to replace our free will with His will!

Another possibility is that we feel that somehow we have sinned beyond anything that God will forgive. Let's go back to the second chapter of Acts but include the two verses before verse 38.

> *Therefore let the entire house of Israel know with certainty that God has made him both Lord and Messiah, this Jesus whom you crucified. Now when they heard this, they were cut to the heart and said to Peter and to the other apostles, "Brothers, what should we do?" Peter said to them, "Repent, and be baptized every one of you in the name of Jesus Christ so that your sins may be forgiven; and you will receive the gift of the Holy Spirit."*
> (Acts 2:36-38).

If Peter told those who had participated in the crucifixion of Christ that they could be forgiven, certainly there is nothing that we have done that, with true repentance, cannot be forgiven by God so that we also may receive the Holy Spirit.

Listen to God

On the other hand, if we feel that we have received the Holy Spirit but still do not know what God's plan is for us, we need to listen to God. We need to pray. We need to study the Bible. We need to be with other persons who know God with whom we can learn and pray. We need to be open to and aware of God's message all around us. Chapter 4 of Acts shows us the power of being in a group of believers.

> *When they had prayed, the place in which they were gathered together was shaken; and they were all filled with the Holy Spirit and spoke the word of God with boldness* (Acts 4:31).

The setting for this verse was in Jerusalem, when the apostles were under great persecution. To speak the word of God with boldness was taking their life into their hands. I do not think that many of us fear losing our lives by witnessing our belief in God, but we may fear that those around us will not approve. So the question we need to answer is: if we are truly doing what God wants us to do and are empowered by the Holy Spirit, what other approvals do we desire? We just need to make sure that it is God's work and not just our ideas about which we "speak boldly."

Trust the Holy Spirit

The following story about two people demonstrates what knowing that you have the Holy Spirit in your life can do for you. One is a Christian who has received the Holy Spirit's power, and the other is a follower of the Islamic faith. They both believe in God, but the Muslim does not believe that Christ is his personal savior, nor does he believe in the indwelling of the Holy Spirit. Knowing that the Holy Spirit empowers him allows the Christian to speak boldly about his life with Christ. The story starts with a Biblical quote that tells us having the Holy Spirit active in our lives will set us apart.

Two Friends

My sheep listen to My voice; I know them, and they follow Me (John 10:27).

Two friends, a Christian and a Muslim, were on a business trip together in a city where neither had previously visited. One afternoon, they were walking together, and the Christian, Frank, wanted to share the gospel with the Muslim, Abdul-Hakeem. As neither knew much of the other's belief, they agreed that each would share their faith with the other. As they walked along, Abdul was knowledgeable about his faith. He started first and dominated the conversation. Frank listened and realized that he would not be as eloquent in describing his belief system as Abdul was. So,

Frank asked the Holy Spirit how he should share his faith with Abdul-Hakeem.

"Do you consider your god your father who speaks to you?" asked Frank.

"Certainly not," replied Abdul.

"That is one of the big differences between your god and my God," said Frank. "I consider that my God speaks to me personally. We converse with each other."

"You can say that, but you cannot prove that," stated Abdul.

Frank again prayed silently: "Lord, how do I prove to this man that as the Holy Spirit, you are always with me. We talk, and you are the source of the truth in my understanding of God?"

Frank and Abdul began approaching two young women coming toward them on the sidewalk a few moments later. As they approached, Frank spoke to the women and made small talk. He then said to one woman, "I believe you are a nurse, is that correct?"

The woman was startled that a man she had never met had just informed her of her occupation. "How would you know that? I have never met you before," she said.

Frank replied, "I asked the Holy Spirit, and He told me." Abdul-Hakeem had his proof.

The basic facts of the story related above are true; the encounter did happen. The Christian man I called Frank did ask for, rely on, and receive inspiration from the Holy Spirit that his witness could be substantial. Have you ever experienced the reality of the Holy Spirit like these two persons? Either in your own life or the life of someone close to you. Many of us do not hear God's voice because we have not accepted the Holy Spirit in our lives and do not believe that God, as the Holy Spirit, will direct our daily lives. If we are to hear the Holy Spirit talk to us, first, we must believe that He will speak to us, and second, we must listen. We must also remember that just knowing and accepting Christ is not necessarily the same as "receiving the Holy Spirit." We could be in the same condition as the new Christians in Samaria.

> *Now when the apostles at Jerusalem heard that Samaria had accepted the word of God, they sent Peter and John to them. The two went down and prayed for them that they might receive the Holy Spirit (for as yet, the Spirit had not come upon any of them; they had only been baptized in the name of the Lord Jesus). Then Peter and John laid their hands on them, and they received the Holy Spirit* (Acts 8:14-17).

Give God Permission

Through prayer, we need to permit God to replace our free will with His will! Then the Holy Spirit can empower us with His gifts, and we will have a complete understanding of God's unconditional and unlimited love for each individual and the knowledge that we have indeed been "born from above."

Keep Track of God's Revelations to You

Make a note in your prayer journal about your prayer that God replaces your free will with His will for your life. Keep track of the revelations that God gives you about what He wants you to do with your life. Also, note how you received each revelation and how you verified that it was from God. Expect the gifts of the Spirit, which are the fourth promise.

Discussion:

1. Do you want the Power of The Holy Spirit in your life?

    a. Are you ready to have God replace your free will with His will? _____

    b. How did or would your life change after receiving the Holy Spirit? _____

    _____

    _____

2. What connotations does the word REPENT have for you? _____

    _____

    a. Are they Positive or Negative? _____

3. What do you think about Acts 2:4? *"All of them were filled with the Holy Spirit and began to speak in other languages, as the Spirit gave them ability."* _____

    _____

4. Does it seem to you that the Holy Spirit is less evident in people's lives today than it was in the time of the early church? _____

    a. If so, why do you think it is less evident? _____

    _____

    b. Give some examples of the Holy Spirit acting in others today. _____

    _____

5. List the times in your life when you felt the presence of the Holy Spirit the most. _____

    _____

    a. Why do you think your awareness of His presence was more vital at these times? _____

    _____

6. Do you believe that a "water baptism" is a pre-requisite to receiving the Holy Spirit? _____

7. What do you believe about infant baptism? _____

    _____

    a. Is it required because of "original sin?" _____

    b. Is it more of a dedication? _____

    c. Is it even required? _____

8. Note how and when you were baptized and what effect it has had on your life. _____

    _____

Call to Action:

1. Permit God to replace your free will with His will!
   Write the date when you first made the petition to God. ___

2. Make a note in your prayer journal about asking God to
   replace your free will with His will for your life.

3. Keep track of the revelations that God gives you about
   what He wants you to do with your life. Along with the
   specific disclosures, note how you received each
   revelation and how you verified that it was from God.

Reading List, Gifts of the spirit:

Acts 2:1-13   1 Corinthians 12:1 through 14:33

Matthew 18:1-5   Romans 12:1-13

Additional Scripture references:

_____

_____

Chapter 4, Gifts of the Spirit

Do you know the difference between being involved and being committed? Think of breakfast, including ham and eggs. The chicken was involved; the pig was committed!

In this chapter, the people I will talk about were not just involved in their Christianity; they were committed to following Christ! They understood God's unconditional love, they knew what it meant to be "born from above," and they gave their lives for their beliefs!

Pentecost

The referenced scriptures for this chapter, Romans 12:1-13 and 1 Corinthians 12:1-14:33, discuss several aspects of "gifts of the Spirit." Paul talks about them in at least three places in his Epistles. Luke introduces us to the Gifts of the spirit in the book of Acts at the time of Pentecost. Let us go back and refresh our memories about what happened at Pentecost, fifty days after Christ's resurrection, as recorded in the second chapter of Acts.

When the day of Pentecost came, they were all together in one place. Suddenly, a sound like the blowing of a violent wind came from heaven and filled the whole house where they were sitting. They saw what seemed to be tongues of fire that separated and came to rest on each of them. All of them were filled with the Holy Spirit and began to speak in other tongues as the Spirit enabled them (Acts 2:1-4, NIV).

Speaking in tongues at Pentecost was the first gift of the Spirit the disciples received. That fact is probably why some Christians have concluded that unless you speak in tongues, you have not received any spiritual gifts, and perhaps, not even received the Holy Spirit.

However, we need to read the following two verses to get the entire story about speaking in tongues.

Now there were staying in Jerusalem God-fearing Jews from every nation under heaven. When they heard this sound, a crowd came together in bewilderment, because each one heard them speaking in his own language (Acts 2:5-6, NIV).

Understanding

The gift received at Pentecost was not just that the apostles were uttering sounds that were unintelligible to each other. The other gift of the Spirit was that they were heard and understood in the native language of each person present. In other words, there was an interpreter for each of the tongues spoken. The Holy Spirit was a translator for all languages spoken there that day! There was no question that the reason the apostles were speaking in languages they did not understand was that it was God's desire for each person in that room to hear the message in the language they understood best. The Holy Spirit had empowered both the lips of the apostles and the listeners' ears so that could happen. The first evidence of the Gifts of the Spirit was very dramatic and very effective.

The reason that the gift of tongues and the gift of interpretation were the first gifts received at Pentecost was not because they are the greatest gifts. Neither are these gifts some qualifier you need before you can receive any other gifts of the

Spirit. The Holy Spirit gave the gifts of tongues and interpretation to the apostles at Pentecost because they were the gifts that the apostles needed that day to be the most effective in presenting the message God intended.

Converted Pagans

Now try to imagine that you lived in Corinth around AD57 when Paul wrote his letters to the Corinthians. Only a little more than 20 years after Christ's crucifixion, His resurrection, and then Pentecost. You have just discovered and accepted Christ in your life, and you are living within a Christian community, a very excited Christian community, a very committed Christian community! Your every thought is about your new life in Christ. However, your background is pagan. You are a Gentile, converted from the practices of pagan worship.

People all around you are practicing their gifts of the Spirit, and you are eager to do this also. People are prophesying, there are healings, and many are converting to Christianity every day. There is much encouragement, teaching, and generosity. Some are speaking in tongues, and many do not have an interpreter!

A Litmus Test

In Corinth, there has been a problem with some of the new believers comparing their spiritual gifts. They believed that some gifts were better than others. Moreover, as some still believe today, they believed that if you had not received a particular gift, the gift of speaking in tongues, maybe you had not received the Holy Spirit!

The Corinthians seemed to be particularly enamored with "speaking in tongues." Undoubtedly, it seemed more like the way they had worshiped their pagan gods and probably because it happened at Pentecost. It must have been awe-inspiring to hear the story of Pentecost related. The idea that the apostles could speak in a language they did not know, and those listening could understand their words as their native language, is beyond what anyone would consider normal! The events that took place at Pentecost were unmistakable evidence of the Holy Spirit. However, it seems that many had forgotten about the interpretation part. They were just babbling, and sometimes, several at once.

The Common Good

In the twelfth chapter of 1 Corinthians, Paul is about to set them straight about Spiritual gifts. The following is a paraphrase of what Paul said.

You need to understand some things about Spiritual gifts. Different gifts do not come from different gods, as you believed when you were pagans. There are different kinds of gifts, but only one Spirit. There are different kinds of service, but the same Lord. Our one God provides the power for all different types of works in all people. Another thing that you must understand, God has given us the gifts of the Spirit to use for the common good. If you are using your Spiritual gifts to divide, you are misusing them!

The Spirit may choose to give you the message of wisdom, or the message of knowledge, or faith, or gifts of healing, or miraculous powers, or prophecy, or the ability to distinguishing between good and evil Spirits, all of these gifts are from one Spirit. This same Spirit may also decide to give you the ability to speak in different kinds of tongues, and to another, the ability to interpret those tongues.

One Spirit and one source of power, the Holy Spirit, decides who gets which gifts. Our option is to accept or reject any gifts the Holy Spirit offers and how we use them if accepted.

The gifts are different, but just like other parts of our bodies, the arm is not better than the leg, nor is the leg better than the ear. All are different, all are important, and all are necessary for various tasks and situations. Paul is precise about how we must use Spiritual gifts. He tells the Corinthians, you must only use your Spiritual gifts for the *good of the community*, and never in a way that divides the community.

The Love Chapter

The thirteenth chapter of 1 Corinthians is one of the favorite and most-read chapters in the New Testament. You probably recognize it as the "Love Chapter." It talks about the things that love is, and the things that love is not. Ministers and others read it at weddings, funerals, and many other occasions. Do you remember how it starts?

If I speak in the tongues of men and of angels, but have not love, I am only a resounding gong or a clanging cymbal (1 Cor. 13:1, NIV).

Hmm, verse 1 starts by talking about speaking in tongues of angels, but seldom is it mentioned that this "Love Chapter" is part of Paul's dissertation about the proper and improper use of the gifts of the Spirit. Paul tells us that all Spiritual gifts come from the same source. They all have merit. However, there are times when each is appropriate, and there are times when each may be inappropriate!

The Appropriate Gift

There is a story about a little boy helping his neighbor that illustrates this very well.

Turner and Mr. Wilson

Mr. Wilson lived next door to a 6-year-old little boy named Turner. Mr. Wilson had lost his wife of 60 years only a few days before, and it had only been three days since the funeral. Mr. Wilson was sitting on his front porch, and Turner was playing in his yard. As Turner looked up from his playing, he noticed that Mr. Wilson was sitting on his porch and looked lonely and maybe a little sad. Turner went over, climbed up on Mr. Wilson's lap, and sat there for quite some time.

Turner's mother noticed her son sitting on Mr. Wilson's lap and was curious about what they were doing. When her son returned, she asked him about what he and Mr. Wilson had been saying to each other. Turner said, "We didn't talk about anything; I just sat on his lap and helped him cry."

Mr. Wilson did not need prophecy, or the utterance of great wisdom, or knowledge. And it was not the time for speaking in tongues. It was the time for the gift of healing. Not that He needed physical healing or even spiritual healing. The gift that the little boy gave so freely that day was the gift of compassionate healing. That came from Turner's spirit understanding that sometimes there is an emptiness that only God's love can fill. This little boy was the conduit that God had chosen to bring the message of love from God to Mr. Wilson by helping him cry.

There is a proper time and place for each of us to allow God to use those spiritual gifts He has given to each true believer. Do you question whether a child can be a true believer or whether God may give gifts of the Spirit to a small child? I believe God will use all of His creation to communicate His love to us. In this case, a child was the best vehicle, and God gave him the necessary gift.

Child-Like

As Christian adults, we certainly do not have any corner on receiving God's spiritual gifts. Although the Scripture does not talk about any children that may have been at Pentecost, Christ tells us that unless we come to Him with the spirit of a child, we will not enter the kingdom of heaven. Verses 1-4 of Matthew 18 specifically list humility as a desirable child-like characteristic. In William Barkley's commentary on Matthew, he lists two other child-like features, dependence and trust. The word openness, which implies humility and trust, seems the best word to describe the characteristic that enabled Turner to minister to Mr. Wilson. The story indicates how the openness that children generally have and adults have often lost can be crucial to our being able to receive and use the gifts of the Spirit. You could also say that since children are used to being dependent upon their parents, it is easier for them to depend upon God in situations like the one in this story and, therefore, easier to allow God's gifts to flow through them.

The story told in Matthew 18:1-4 is about the disciples asking Jesus who is the greatest. There seems to be a constant theme about position and greatness that concerned the disciples. In the tenth chapter of Mark, James and John want to be first and second after Christ. It is not surprising; the disciples were ordinary people, just like us today before Christ called them. They were interested in how they compared to each other as disciples and others in their communities.

Today when we make that comparison, we usually use the word success. How successful are you in your job, in your investments, at your leisure? What is your handicap in golf? What school did you attend? We even talk about the success of one church relative to another by comparing the buildings, the size of the congregation, or the size of the annual budget.

Change Your Way of Thinking

As was usually the case, when the disciples asked a question about their success, Christ answered with an example, a parable, that would cause them to change their way of thinking about themselves and their relationship to God. Christ designed the parable to encourage them to forget about the comparisons between perceived human values and concentrate on the fundamental values, the eternal values. These examples are timeless and today help to make us think about how we relate to God!

Let us listen to the conversation recorded in Matthew between Christ and the disciples.

The disciples asked, "Who is the greatest in the kingdom of heaven?"

Christ looked around and saw a little child. He called the child to come and stand with the group and said:

"I am going to tell you something that you may find hard to believe, but unless you change and start looking at the world like this little child and have the openness and humility of this child, you will never enter the kingdom of heaven. And you must not ignore this child or act like he is unimportant because whoever welcomes this child welcomes me."

Proper Value System

Christ is telling His disciples that the child's value system is better than the value system of the disciples. And that all persons, regardless of age, have value to Him. He also tells the disciples they should be careful to treat everyone as important because all persons are important to Christ. I believe this should eliminate any of our doubts about whether God may empower a child with a special gift of the Spirit.

Let us return to Paul's instructions relative to the use of the gifts of the Spirit. It will help us get a better perspective on what Paul thought were the proper measures of success or failure. Paul does not believe that all gifts of the Spirit are appropriate at all times. He also indicates that there are rules for using the gifts of the Spirit. In the twelfth chapter of Romans, he states that not all will receive the same gifts.

> *For by the grace given to me I say to everyone*
> *among you not to think of yourself more highly than*
> *you ought to think, but to think with sober judgment,*
> *each according to the measure of faith that God has*

assigned. For as in one body we have many members, and not all the members have the same function, so we, who are many, are one body in Christ, and individually we are members one of another. We have gifts that differ according to the grace given to us: prophecy, in proportion to faith; ministry, in ministering; the teacher, in teaching; the exhorter, in exhortation; the giver, in generosity; the leader, in diligence; the compassionate, in cheerfulness (Rom. 12:3-8).

The gifts of the Spirit that each of us receives are likely to enhance or use talents God has already given us. For instance, if God had given us the talent to be a good speaker, we might expect the gift of Prophecy from the Holy Spirit. Paul reminds us that the rule for our use of the gift of Prophecy is that it must be in proportion to our faith. When we group statements about and lists of the different gifts of the Spirit that Paul talks about, we reinforce the idea that the gifts of the Spirit are primarily – God's empowerment of a skill, a talent, or a personality characteristic that we already have, to a much higher level. For instance, in addition to the gifts of speaking in tongues, prophesying, and interpreting, Paul also talks about gifts of wisdom, serving, teaching, healing, encouraging, contributing to the needs of others, leadership, showing mercy, faith, miraculous powers, and distinguishing between spirits (good and evil). Each of us has at least one of these capabilities. However, with the Holy Spirit's gifts in our lives, we are much more effective in using these talents. Paul also indicates that we should desire all of the Holy Spirit's gifts and be ready to accept and use them if the Holy Spirit gives them to us. However, Paul reminds us there is an overriding directive for using any gift of the Holy Spirit. These gifts must only be used to strengthen the Christian community, never to divide it. Also, we must use them within our level of understanding, for example, prophecy in proportion to our faith.

His Will, Not Ours

We must not go off on our own, misusing a gift that the Holy Spirit has given us. As always, we need to wait for the Holy Spirit and allow the Spirit to guide us in everything we do. Prayer, study, discussion within our Christian community, and reason are essential in determining the proper use of any of God's gifts we have received. These are all methods that the Holy Spirit uses to guide us. The need for receiving guidance from the Holy Spirit is especially true of those gifts that allow us to act as God's agent with His power in our lives. We must always make sure that it is for His will that we are using these gifts and not our own.

List Your Gifts

Go back in your journal and examine what you have recorded about God's revelation of His will for your life. Are there gifts of the Holy Spirit that you have received that you feel are necessary for you to do His will? If so, write in your journal how you are using those gifts for the tasks God has given you. If you feel you need additional gifts to accomplish the tasks God has given you, list those gifts. Also, note how you think these gifts will help you with the tasks God has asked you to do. Finally, pray about receiving those gifts you feel you need, asking God whether He agrees you need them.

Discussion:

1. How do you think that the "gifts of the Holy Spirit" should be manifested in people today? _____

   _____

2. Are you aware of any of the gifts of the Holy Spirit in people you know? _____

   a. List any that you believe you have observed. _____

   _____

   b. How did you become aware of them? _____

   _____

3. Have you ever felt threatened by someone who you thought had received any of the gifts of the Holy Spirit?

   _____

   a. What was it that made you feel threatened? _____

   _____

4. After reading this chapter and the related scriptures, have you changed your mind about which "gifts of the Holy Spirit" you think you have or want? Then, put a checkmark beside those you desire.

   The gift of wisdom _____

   The gift of knowledge _____

   The gift of serving _____

   The gift of teaching _____

   Contributing to the needs of others _____

   The gift of faith _____

   The gift of healing _____

   Miraculous powers, _____

   The gift of prophecy _____

distinguishing between Spirits, _____

speaking in tongues, _____

interpretation of tongues _____

5. From the list above, how would each of those that you checked change your life? _____

_____

_____

_____

6. List the gifts of the Holy Spirit that you think you have:

_____

_____

   a. How have these changed your life? _____

_____

_____

_____

Call to Action:

1. Go back in your journal and examine what you have recorded about God's revelation of His will for your life. List the gifts of the Holy Spirit that you have received that you feel are necessary for you to do His will. _____

   _____

   _____

2. List in your journal how you are using, or intend to use, those gifts for the tasks that God has given you.

3. If you feel you need additional gifts to accomplish the tasks God has given you, list those gifts in your journal and summarize them here. _____

   _____

   _____

4. Note in your journal how you think these gifts will help you with the tasks that God is asking you to do.

5. Pray about receiving those gifts you feel you need, asking God whether He agrees that you need them.

Reading List, Grace:

2 Corinthians 12:1-10   John 1:1-18
Acts 15:1-12   Romans 3:9-26
Matthew 5:17-48   Romans 5:12 through 6:11

Additional Scripture references:

_____

_____

Chapter 5, Grace

The following story is a practical example of why we should all be interested in God's grace.

Mom's Little Helper

A woman invited some people to a dinner party. After a full day of preparation, she was ready. With the guests all seated around the table, she turned to her six-year-old daughter and said, "Would you like to say the blessing?"

"I don't know what to say," the little girl replied.

"Just say what you have heard Mommy say," answered the mother.

The daughter bowed her head and said, "Lord, why on earth did I invite all these people to dinner?"

While this event certainly was not a major catastrophe in the mother's life, it demonstrates that we often say things that can bring hurt into our lives and those around us. However, God's Grace is available for both the small and large problems in our lives.

God Decides

Is there a conflict between the concepts of "Gifts of the Spirit" and "Grace?" On the one hand, we have the gifs of healing and performing miracles, and on the other, we have grace sufficient for any need. Paul had a lot to say about grace. Chapter 12 of 2 Corinthians talks of his own need for grace because of an ailment, his thorn in the flesh, which will not go away.

> *Therefore, to keep me from being too elated, a thorn was given me in the flesh, a messenger of Satan to torment me, to keep me from being too elated. Three times I appealed to the Lord about this, that it would leave me, but he said to me, "My grace is sufficient for you, for power is made perfect in weakness"*... (2 Cor. 12:7b-9).

God will not give us a burden beyond the grace that He has given us. Paul and the other apostles were able to heal many persons with both spiritual and physical ills. However, there was some reason that God chose not to cure this problem of Paul's, his thorn in the side, or there was something in Paul's life that was blocking the healing. Paul believed it was the former; God had chosen not to heal him, and the reason was to keep Paul from being too proud. However, God said that His grace was sufficient for Paul to live his life according to God's plan. We need to make sure that we understand what God told Paul. God did not say that He would provide the grace to enable Paul to do and be whatever Paul wanted. No, Paul wanted God to take the affliction away. God did say that He would provide the grace necessary for Paul to live his life *according to God's plan.*

Grace Over Healing

God decided not to heal Paul's "thorn in the side," but He gave Paul the strength and the understanding that he needed to be the person God wanted Paul to be. He even let Paul know why He made the decision not to heal this affliction. That is how complete God's grace is if we allow God to take over our free will. There is a time for healing, and there is a time for grace to overcome. We need to recognize that it is not our choice; the decision and the timing belong to God. I am not saying that we give up easily on praying for healing. Paul said that he asked three times. I am saying that we need to listen to God and accept His decision on the proper solution to our problems.

In the fourth Gospel, John starts by saying, *"In the beginning was the Word."* He continues by saying, the Word "Christ" was a part of all creation, that John is the witness to Christ, and that Christ is the incarnation of God as man.

> *The Word became flesh and made his dwelling among us. We have seen his glory, the glory of the One and Only, who came from the Father, full of grace and truth* (John 1:14, NIV).

John, the witness to Christ, tells us that Christ, God incarnate, was full of grace. I suppose that we would expect that, with Christ being God. However, the significance is not that as God incarnate, Christ was full of grace; the significance is that as a human, Christ was full of grace.

Christ was both fully God and fully human. God is the source of grace, but Christ, as a human, required grace, and John tells us that He *was* full of grace. Throughout the New Testament, Paul tells us that grace is the gift from God that sustains us through the problems that arrive from our humanness and is our source of salvation. The verse used to start the first chapter of this book, John 3:16, tells us grace is the source of our salvation. God gave His only son that through His grace, we could receive salvation. Another way God demonstrates His unconditional love for us. When we accept

God's grace, we learn more about what it means to be "born from above."

Must I be Jewish First?

Chapter 15 of Acts reveals that some in the church at Antioch said that contrary to what Paul had said, to be a Christian, you first had to be a Jew. So, therefore, circumcision was required for all males in the tradition of Moses. And that was just one of the more obvious rules that they wanted to apply.

You see, there were both Jews and Gentiles in the church at Antioch. For the Jews, being a Christian was primarily accepting that Christ was the Messiah their scriptures had predicted. Therefore, it made sense that being a Jew was the appropriate starting point to be a Christian. However, this was in conflict with what Paul had told the Gentile-Christians, so Paul gets more specific!

He tells these Jewish-Christians that trying to follow the Mosaic Law did not work before, so why would you require it now? He said being a Jew is great. Additionally, he said, I am a Jew, and Christ was a Jew. However, there is a new covenant in Christ, and we can start today from where we are today. We do not have to go back and try to be a Jew first. To say otherwise is trying God's patience.

Paul told the Jewish-Christians: the Mosaic Law was a yoke that neither our ancestors nor we have ever been able to bear! He told them not only do the new gentile-Christians not have to be circumcised; to state otherwise is "putting God to the test!" Then he added, as Jews that have accepted Christ, you should know better! We cannot earn our salvation; what we do physically to our bodies is not the source of our salvation. Our salvation will come only through God's Saving Grace, which He freely gives to all believers.

No One Can be Righteous by the Law

Were the Jewish-Christians at Antioch particularly hard-headed? Maybe they thought that the Gentile-Christians were getting a free ride. Hey, if I lived all my life trying to follow the Mosaic Law, does it not make sense, as a minimum, to require circumcision for the Gentiles? Sort of an entry fee to make sure they are serious. After all, this was the symbol that we had accepted our part of the covenant with God!

Well, this was not just a problem for the Christians at Antioch. Paul's letter to the Romans tells them: God can not declare you righteous because you followed the law. We are human, and humans sin. We rebel against God, we miss His purpose for our life, and we surrender to the power of evil rather than to God!

Whoops! Maybe these Christians at Antioch and Rome are not that different from us! We certainly are human, and we certainly do sin, at least I do. There may also be a certain amount of trying to earn salvation as well. Paul then tells the Christians in Rome—and us today, if we listen—that God declares us righteous only through His grace. Let us listen to how Paul put it in the third chapter of his letter to the Romans—it is a good news / bad news story. In this case, the Bad News came first.

God will not declare anyone righteous in His sight through the observance of the law. The law only makes us conscious of sin. However, since Christ, there is a new righteousness from God, apart from the law. The scriptures that you have tell you about it. This righteousness from God comes through faith in Jesus Christ to all who believe!

All Have Sinned

Paul is not done yet; here is the kicker:

There is no difference whether Greek or Jew, "for all have sinned and fallen short of the glory of God."

That is the Bad News. All have sinned, the prophets and everyone who ever lived that was "born of man." That excludes only Christ; Jews do not have a head start on the Gentiles. Everyone is starting from square one.

However, as Paul continues with the Good News, he tells us:

Even though we have sinned, <u>we are justified freely by His grace through the redemption that came by Christ Jesus.</u> God has presented Christ as our sacrifice of atonement if we have faith and accept this gift.

Then Paul closes by saying:

Man is justified by faith, apart from observing the law.

Well, that is a little like good news / bad news again. If I have lived a relatively good life, the bad news is that nothing I did before I accepted Christ affects where and how I will spend eternity! On the other hand, if you have lived a less than stellar life, the good news is that nothing I did before I accepted Christ affects where and how I will spend eternity!

We are new persons in Christ. We have acknowledged and repented of our sins of the past. We believe that Christ has made the ultimate sacrifice for all of our sins. We are beginning to accept God's grace in our life. We are starting to believe that "His grace is sufficient" for all our needs! We are beginning to believe that God gave His Son so that we (each of us individually) can have everlasting life with Him.

Fulfill the Law

Now, wait just a minute, didn't Christ say that He did not come to eliminate the law?

> *Do not think that I have come to abolish the law or the prophets; I have come not to abolish but to fulfill* (Matt. 5:17).

I do not understand; I am confused. First, we learn that Paul said that the law did not do anything but convict people.

68

He tells us the sacrifice of Christ was a gift for our personal salvation. However, Matthew records that Christ appears to have said that the law is still significant sometime before Paul wrote his letters. What was Christ referring to when He said the law or the prophets? Well, this is a reference to the Hebrew Scriptures—the Bible that Christ used. The Jews identified these Scriptures in several different ways. Sometimes the scriptures were called The Torah, but frequently the name used identified their content—"The books of the Law and the books of the Prophets." The latter identification is customarily shortened to simply "The Law and The Prophets."

Therefore, what Christ said He came to fulfill was: <u>God's promises found in what we call the Old Testament</u>. By fulfilling those promises—through His teaching, His examples, His suffering, and His death and resurrection—and by being the promised Messiah, He removed the hold that the law and sin had on people. Now, through the Holy Spirit, we have God's grace to take away our trespasses.

New Covenant

In Paul's preaching and writings, he told the new Christians that Christ had fulfilled the Old Testament promises, and He had fulfilled the old covenant. Therefore, the old covenant is obsolete and has been replaced with the new covenant. The new covenant only requires us to accept the grace given by God. Well, that is good news. A lot better than I ever thought it could be. I do as I please right up to the last minute and then call upon God's grace for salvation! I get to have it both ways—you can hardly beat that!

Died to Sin

Well, not so fast. Paul had something to say about that also. He told the Christians in Rome:

The law was added so that the trespass might increase. But where sin increased, grace increased

69

all the more, so that, just as sin reigned in death, so also grace might reign through righteousness to bring eternal life through Jesus Christ our Lord. What shall we say, then? Shall we go on sinning so that grace may increase? By no means! We died to sin; how can we live in it any longer? (Rom. 5:20-6:2, NIV).

We died to sin; how can we live in it any longer? Bummer, Paul just will not leave us alone. Even Paul, who could be called Mr. 'Faith not Works' or Mr. 'Grace not the Law,' has an answer for why we will still want to try to follow God's rules. You see, even though the law has no hold upon us in the sense that it cannot keep us from salvation, we will not consciously want to break God's law because we love Him.

Besides, let's get practical. Why would we consciously want to go against God's will in our lives when He has promised us the power, through His grace, to be able to handle all situations that come up? All we need to do is believe, have faith, and accept the Holy Spirit! Without question, that is a power that everyone would like to have in their life, isn't it?

That is "The Good News." That is "The Gospel."

Just think of it. The availability of God's grace and the Holy Spirit's power is the most powerful message of the New Testament. There is no need to worry. God is on top of everything. However, we have to be ready to accept God's solution to every problem! Like Paul did!

Do God's Will

Yes, it is true. God will not give us a burden beyond the grace that He has given us. However, there is a catch. We have to be working on doing God's will in our lives. That means that we have to find out what His will is for us. We do that using Prayer, study, discipline, and patience! Then, after receiving His answer and understanding what His will is for us, there must be action.

God does not work on our schedule! God does not rubber-stamp what we think His will should be!

As I said in the chapter on gifts of the Holy Spirit, if we want to live our lives to the fullest, in the marvelous way God has planned for us, we must understand and apply the scripture in the sixth chapter of Matthew.

Seek ye **first** the kingdom of God and His righteousness, and all these things will be added unto you.

All these things – Including His all-sufficient grace.

God's Plan(s)

There we are, right back to the beginning, the overriding aspect of our relationship with God. He wants to be first in our lives! He demands to be first in our lives! However, He does not force this. He has given us free will. We can mess up our lives beyond recognition of what God wants for us. God has had a plan for each one of us since the beginning of time. From the time we were born, we have made some choices that brought us closer to God and other decisions that have taken us farther from God.

The neat thing, the really very neat thing, is that God already has a new plan that will bring us back to Him even before we mess up. That, in part, is how His grace works. We cannot do anything that His grace cannot handle. Besides, we cannot create a separation from Him that His plan for us will not close.

In reality, we only have two choices. We can trust our capabilities, make our own decisions, deny that our talents and skills came from God, and live with the consequences. On the other hand, we can trust in God, ask for His help in our decisions, be patient in waiting for His answer, and have the infinite power of God in our lives.

The following story about a boy and his father shows one aspect of our choices and the consequences of the wrong choice. The choice was letting a bad temper control the boy or for the boy to control his temper. In this story, a wise earthly father helped the boy understand the difference in the choices and the consequences.

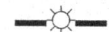

The Fence

There was a little boy who had a bad temper. His father gave him a bag of nails and told him that he must hammer a nail into the back of the fence every time he lost his temper. The first day the boy had driven 37 nails into the fence. Over the next few weeks, as he learned to control his anger, the number of nails hammered daily gradually dwindled. He discovered it was easier to hold his temper than to drive those nails into the fence. Finally, the day came when the boy did not lose his temper at all. He told his father about it and, the father suggested that the boy now pull out one nail for each day that he was able to hold his temper.

The days passed, and the young boy finally told his father that all the nails were gone. The father took his son by the hand and led him to the fence. He said, "You have done well, my son, but look at the holes in the fence. The fence will never be the same. When you say things in anger, they leave a scar just like this one. You can put a knife in a man and draw it out. It will not matter how many times you say I am sorry; the wound is still there. A verbal wound is as bad as a physical one.

The holes are not just in other people's fences; the holes are also in God's fence! Which choices have you been making? Are you choosing to seek the kingdom of God first, or are you seeking and attempting to build your kingdom on this earth?

Are you storing up your treasures on earth, where moth and rust destroy, and where thieves break in and steal, or are you storing up your treasures in heaven?

Start Now

Would you like to change your choices? Start today, start now, and make God the priority in your life. Seek His kingdom without reservation. Spend sufficient time in prayer to find His will for you. Accept His grace and salvation in your life, and let God show you the marvelous things He has planned for you for eternity. In the gift of God's grace, we see His unconditional love again. As we accept God's grace operating in our lives, we will truly understand the meaning of "being born from above."

Discussion:

1. Have you ever felt that you have received a burden that was beyond the grace that God has given you to handle that burden? _____

   a. Describe the situation _____

   _____

   b. Why did you feel the burden was beyond the grace received? _____

   _____

2. Does Paul's explanation of why God did not grant his requested healing satisfy you? _____

3. How do you know whether you should expect the power from the Holy Spirit to take away or solve a problem, or if you should ask for the grace of God to sustain you through the trouble? _____

   _____

4. List the most essential areas in your life where you need God's grace.

   a. Family relationships _____

   _____

   b. Personal relationships outside the family _____

   _____

   c. Economic problems _____

   _____

   d. Other problems _____

   _____

Call to Action:

1. Start today, start now, and make God the priority in your life.

2. Seek His kingdom without reservation.

3. Spend the time in prayer that it takes to find His will for you.

4. Accept His grace and salvation in your life, and let God show you the marvelous things He has planned for you for eternity.

5. Let His grace help you truly understand the meaning of "being born from above."

Reading List, All Things for Good:

Romans 8:28-39   Mark 14:32-42
Matthew 19:16-26   Matthew 7:7-12

Additional Scripture references:

_____

_____

Chapter 6, All Things for Good

Chapter 8 of Romans identifies the sixth promise related to God's unlimited love. Paul is contrasting the "Spiritual Life" with a life that follows our "natural inclinations." Here, as in several other places, Paul tells us *that if we have accepted Christ and allowed the Holy Spirit to control us*, that is, if we have been born from above, neither the Mosaic Law, nor sin, has any hold on our lives. Our bodies have died to sin and, we are alive in Christ. What's more, everything that happens in our lives, God turns to our good!

> *And we know that in all things God works for the good of those who love him, who have been called according to his purpose* (Rom. 8:28, NIV).

God and Suffering

The question is, how does God work in our lives? Is God only responsible for the good things in our lives? Does He just *allow* the terrible things? Relative to Christ and His suffering, His prayer in the Garden of Gethsemane certainly relates that Christ believes that God is in control of the entire event: scourging, crucifixion, death, and resurrection.

> *And going a little farther, he threw himself on the ground and prayed that, if it were possible, the hour might pass from him. He said, "Abba, Father, for you all things are possible; remove this cup*

from me; yet, not what I want, but <u>what you want</u>" (Mark 14:35-36).

Since we know that Christ did suffer and die on the cross, then based on Christ's prayer, we must conclude that this is what God wanted! Christ dying on the cross was not just something that God allowed sinful men to do. All of this was a part of God's plan. The suffering of Christ on the cross certainly qualifies as the worst that man can do to another to cause suffering. However, God ordained Christ's suffering as payment for our sins so that we could be reconciled to Him. God ordained these acts to save our souls! So why are we taught that the ends do not justify the means? What is different? Why was it acceptable for God to use the horrible death of Christ as the means to the marvelous ends of our salvation? The difference is that God knows the result and the full effect of the actions used to obtain the result. In our case, when we seek to justify an evil deed because we think it will have the desired result, we have neither the knowledge of, nor the control over, the full effect of the evil act. Therefore, we cannot ensure the outcome, nor can we control the potential side effects. As Matthew recorded in Chapter 19:

*But Jesus looked at them and said, "For mortals it is impossible, but for God all things are possible." (*Matt. 19:26).

Do the Ends Justify the Means?

Yes, I know the verse before this talks about a camel passing through the eye of a needle, but it is about salvation. This discussion is also relative to salvation. When we use evil deeds to bring about what we determine to be a good result, we play God, which is sin. Throughout history, the greatest travesties against our fellow man and God have been when individuals or groups have tried to claim and use God's power for their purposes.

78

We must, with God's help, do all we can to refrain from evil. Only God can bring His good out of evil; we cannot achieve good results from evil deeds. God wants to give His children the best in life. However, we often get in His way by taking shortcuts or thinking that God will not provide what we need. Then we go against His will to achieve the results that we desire. In Matthew, Christ said:

> *Ask and it will be given to you;*
>
> *search, and you will find;*
>
> *knock, and the door will be opened to you.*
>
> *Everyone who asks receives; everyone who searches finds; everyone who knocks will have the door opened* (Matt. 7:7-8).

Our Evil Converted to God's Good

If we live within God's will and expect His good gifts, God will provide what we ask for or even better. However, it will be on His schedule. Also, there is nothing that evil can do that God cannot turn to good. What we have to keep in mind is the same thing that Christ said in the Garden of Gethsemane: "*...not what I want, but what you want* (for me)." If we expect God to respond fully to our requests and expect His good to transform the evils that are done to us, then we must strive to live within His will and be willing to wait for His schedule.

As I mentioned in the introduction, the most dramatic example of this was not an event that I observed but in 1917 when my father was eleven. During the last week of my Dad's life, I just began to understand that God was involved in this event. I realized the night Dad died that God had been working in his life for a long time, even though he never talked about it. Dad had claimed the promise given in Romans 8:28 several times. The first time was at age 11 when the doctors amputated his right arm at the shoulder due to an "accident." The second was after he was married when he ran a large spike through his good arm between the elbow and the shoulder. The last of these potentially tragic events in his life was at the age of 65 when he lost two fingers on his remaining hand in a farming accident. Each of these events left my father as a stronger person than he was before the event. The first event was the most dramatic. Without God's intervention, he would have been severely handicapped and unable to perform his life occupation of being a farmer.

Two Choices

There were no functional appliances to replace an entire arm in 1917. Therefore, my father had to make one of two choices. First, he chose to be helpless and let his mother and older sister take care of all of his needs. After this had gone on for several weeks, his dad presented a second choice. Either my dad could continue to be helpless or, he could quit feeling sorry for himself, get up, and do whatever it was that he wanted to do. I know now that God was working in his life, helping him to make that decision. Through God's grace, my dad became a stronger person than he was before he lost his arm. Dad also was a stronger person as an adult because of this event and the resulting decision. Because he made the right choice, he was no longer disabled. He did not consider himself handicapped and, neither did anyone else that ever worked with him.

He farmed in Western Nebraska for his dad until the age of twenty and then for himself for the next 45 years. As a kid working with my dad, I never remember him complaining about only having one arm or using it as an excuse not to do anything. Sometimes he needed to be a little more creative, but he always completed the job. For the very few things that he had trouble with, first my mom, then my sister or I, and later my brother took our turns helping him. I learned several lessons from being around and working with my dad. First, I realized that you did not take shortcuts in life because something you were doing could have been easier if you cut a few corners. Dad was fond of saying: "If it is worth doing, it is worth doing right." He did not just say it—he lived it. Other things I learned while working with my dad were: Be respectful of others, accept people as they are, be helpful whenever possible, and people working together can be more than the sum of each individual separately.

Expectations

I think much of how my dad interacted with people was due to his expectations. He believed that he should treat others at least as well as he would like to be treated. As an example of this, I was taught that if we ever borrowed someone else's equipment, it should be returned in better shape than when it was received, and always with a full tank of gas, regardless of how much it had when it was borrowed. Many of these lessons did not fully sink in until later in my life and, some are still not as firm in my life as they should be. It is not that my dad was a saint; it is just that his relationships with people generally exhibited a deep understanding of how God wanted him to relate to people. He did not talk about his relationship with God—he lived it.

What brought me to understand this was the last event in Dad's life, a fall and a broken hip. This event also seemed to be a tragedy, and I asked God several times why this had to happen. That week, I learned lessons about life and things about my father that I would have never known otherwise. I do not know whether this event was necessary for Dad and his relationship with God. I do know that God changed my relationship with Him that week. God also changed my understanding of how He had worked in and through my dad's life. God was still using my dad to give me another of life's lessons.

A Lost Lamb

A story about a doctor and a young boy shows how situations or events that seem evil or wrong to us can be a part of God's overall plan. Because of our limited viewpoint and limited understanding, we may miss some of God's lessons until He presents them to us through what would be a tragedy without God in our lives.

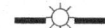

The Heart

"Tomorrow morning," the surgeon began, "I'll open up your heart..."

"You'll find Jesus there," the boy interrupted.

The surgeon looked up, annoyed. "I'll cut your heart open," he continued, "to see how much damage has been done..."

"But when you open up my heart, you'll find Jesus in there," said the boy.

The surgeon looked to the parents, who sat quietly. "When I see how much damage has been done, I'll sew your heart and chest back up, and I'll plan what to do next."

"But you'll find Jesus in my heart. The Bible says He lives there. The hymns all say He lives there. You'll find Him in my heart."

The surgeon had had enough. "I'll tell you what I'll find in your heart. I will find damaged muscle, low blood supply, and weakened vessels. And I'll find out if I can make you well."

"You'll find Jesus there too. He lives there."

The surgeon left.

The surgeon sat in his office, recording his notes from the surgery, "...damaged aorta, damaged pulmonary vein, and widespread muscle degeneration. No hope for transplant, no hope for a cure."

Therapy: "painkillers and bed rest."

Prognosis: here, he paused, "death within one year."

He stopped the recorder, but the surgeon had more to say. "Why?" He asked aloud, "why did You do this?

"You've put him here; You have put him in this pain, and You have cursed him to an early death." "Why?"

The Lord answered and said, "The boy, My lamb, was not meant for your flock for long, for he is a part of My flock, and will forever be. Here he will feel no pain and will be comforted as you cannot imagine. His parents will one day join him here, and they will know peace, and My flock will continue to grow."

The surgeon's tears were hot, but his anger was searing. "You created that boy, and You created that heart. He will be dead in months. Why?"

The Lord answered: "The boy, My lamb, shall return to My flock, for he has done his duty: I did not put My lamb with your flock to lose him, but to retrieve another lost lamb."

The surgeon wept. The surgeon sat beside the boy's bed; the boy's parents sat across from him.

The boy awoke and whispered, "Did you cut open my heart?"

"Yes," said the surgeon.

"What did you find?" asked the boy.

"I found Jesus there," said the surgeon.

God has called each of us to a purpose greater than we understand. How He will bring us to realize this purpose, we do not know. He may create events in our lives that are tragic at first, but we know that if we seek His righteousness, He will transform evil into good for us. Also, know that, just as it required Christ to die on the cross before we could receive the gift of salvation, it will require death to a life of sin in our own lives before we can realize His purpose. It must be His life that lives within us, not our own.

Faith and Understanding

Consider events in your own life; can you see how God has used these events to increase your faith and your understanding of what He wants you to accomplish for Him? Thank God for his unconditional love, for finding ways to change your life for the better when you accept His way and believe in Him, and for His consistency in your life.

Discussion:

1. How do you view Romans 8:28,

    a. Does God cause bad things, like the death of a loved one, so that He can bring good out of it? _____

    b. Alternatively, does God only <u>allow</u> the bad events in our life and then work them to our good? _____

    c. Explain your choice. (Re-read "The Heart," and then re-read the quoted scripture Mark 14:35-36 along with the paragraph that follows on the first page of this chapter.) _____

    _____

    _____

2. Is God involved in war? _____

    a. If so, how do you think God is involved in a war? _

    _____

    _____

3. Is there such a thing as a "Just War?" _____

4. Are you allowing God to do "good works" through you by experiencing the love of God in your life? _____

    a. List some of the "good works" that God is performing through you. _____

    _____

5. List some events where you believe God has brought good out of evil. _____

    _____

Call to Action:

1. Consider events in your own life; can you see how God has used these events to increase your faith and your understanding of what He wants you to accomplish for Him?

2. Make an entry in your journal. List each of these events and describe how they have changed your life. Make this a dynamic list, and add to it each time you recognize something that God has used to improve your ability to serve Him.

3. Thank God for his unconditional love.

4. Thank God for wanting the best for you.

5. Thank God for finding ways to change your life for the better when you accept His way and believe in Him.

Reading List, Consistency:

John 1:1-10   James 1:12-27

Genesis 3:1-13

Additional Scripture references:

_____

_____

Chapter 7, Consistency

Christ, the Word, has existed for all of time and will continue to exist for eternity. You can always count on His existence. It is the ultimate consistency, the constant power in the world, and the continuous gift of His unconditional love.

> *In the beginning, was the Word, and the Word was with God, and the Word was God. He was with God in the beginning. Through him, all things were made; without him, nothing was made that has been made* (John 1:1-3, NIV).

There is no change in God, there has been no change in God, and there will be no change in God!

> *Do not be deceived, my beloved. Every generous act of giving, with every perfect gift, is from above, coming down from the Father of lights, with whom there is no variation or shadow due to change* (James 1:16-17).

The world is full of change. There is an old saying that the only thing that does not change is that everything will change! That is, everything but God! The Bible tells us there is no variation or shadow due to change with God. Why does it appear that the God of the Old Testament is different from the God of the New Testament? We usually talk about the judgment of God the Father in the Old Testament and the Love of Christ, the son in the New Testament. Yet the Gospel of John opens by stating that Christ, the Word, has been with God from the beginning, and in fact, is God.

God Seems to Change

We tend to think that God changes. We see what we believe is a change in God because we change, and therefore, our understanding of God changes. Someone once said that if God seems farther away at times, God is not the one that moved. The same is true relative to our perception that God has changed over time. The change is in our understanding of God and in how we relate to Him. At the beginning of the Old Testament, everything God has created He declares is "good." After He created mankind, God said that it was "very good." God had a straightforward relationship with all of His creation. Adam and Eve wandered around in the garden with all of God's gifts available to them just for the asking. There was only one limitation. <u>Do not eat of the fruit of the tree of knowledge!</u> Again, we learn that although God is always available, we can separate ourselves from Him because He has given us free will. In Other words, we have some responsibilities in this relationship. He is consistent in His love for us, but our actions can make us unable to accept His love and even His salvation.

Be Like God

We do not know precisely how long humankind spent in this blissful state in the Garden of Eden, being at one with God and His creation. However, it was at least long enough for Satan to leave God's ranks and set up his operation because the Bible tells us in Genesis:

> *But the serpent* (Satan) *said to the woman, "You will not die; for God knows that when you eat of it your eyes will be opened, and <u>you will be like God</u>, knowing good and evil"* (Gen. 3:4-5)**.**

That was all that it took, "you will be like God!" Things have not changed that much. Wanting to be God was the original sin that separated man from God, and either wanting to be or acting as though we are God is still one of the most common sins of today. Reading on in Chapter 3 of Genesis, we see the consequences.

> *Then the eyes of both were opened, and they knew that they were naked; and they sewed fig leaves together and made loincloths for themselves. They heard the sound of the LORD God walking in the garden at the time of the evening breeze, and the man and his wife hid themselves from the presence of the LORD God among the trees of the garden. But the LORD God called to the man, and said to him, "Where are you?" He said, "I heard the sound of you in the garden, and I was afraid, because I was naked; and I hid myself." He said, "Who told you that you were naked? Have you eaten from the tree of which I commanded you not to eat?" The man said, "The woman whom you gave to be with me, she gave me fruit from the tree, and I ate." Then the LORD God said to the woman, "What is this that you have done?" The woman said, "The serpent tricked me, and I ate" (Gen. 3:7-13).*

Someone to Blame

They disobeyed God's instructions, and each of them found someone else to blame. Adam blamed Eve, but actually, He was blaming God. He said, "It was the woman that you gave me that caused me to sin." In turn, Eve blamed the snake. In today's language, she would have said, "The devil made me do it." Adam and Eve refused to take responsibility for their actions and then separated themselves from God because of their guilt. We do this to ourselves every time we decide to do something contrary to God's will for us. The consistency of

God's Love for Adam and Eve did not change. It has not changed for us today. Adam and Eve tried to hide from God, and we try to hide today. However, God went looking for them, and He is constantly looking for us today. Not that we can actually hide from God, He always knows where we are. God went looking for Adam and Eve, and He looks for us in a spiritual way. He knows that we have separated ourselves from Him. The verse in Genesis said that God went looking for Adam and Eve. The message is that God is actively working to help us remove whatever is separating us from Him. God does not turn His love for us on and off depending upon what we do. He does not take away His gift of salvation every time we go against His will. His love is unconditional and consistent. Like Adam and Eve, we try to hide, and God is constantly looking, actively working, waiting with open arms, ready with a new plan to return each of us to His grand plan and our salvation. When we do not feel close to God, it is not His fault. It is our own.

How Do We Know

So how do we know when we are operating contrary to God's will? First, we should listen more to our inner thoughts. God created us with a conscience. Our conscience is one of the ways God communicates with us. When our conscience tells us that we should not do something, we probably should not. If we are not sure, we should err on the side of caution. Secondly, we should confide in God. Rather than thinking we can hide from God. We need to seek His counsel on all our decisions. We need to count on the consistency of God for forgiveness of the past and guidance for the future. If we want to claim the promise of His power in our lives, we must be consistent in praying to God, and we must listen for His answers. As I said in Chapter 1, we must have our priorities straight if we want to receive the most of what God is trying to give us. We must be consistent in our search to understand more of what God wants us to do, and the way we do that is through prayer.

God's Power

The following story about the *Columbine Massacre* shows us what has happened and what continues to happen when we ignore God's consistency and the power that it can bring to our lives. It shows the negative side of human behavior, the tendency to sin that has existed in all since Adam and Eve first separated themselves from God. We perform evil acts, we refuse to take responsibility, and we separate ourselves from God. The only way to counteract this force of evil in our life is to avail ourselves of God's consistent power.

Darrell Scott Testimony

The following is an excerpt from Darrell Scott's speech as testimony to the House Judiciary Committee as they were trying to determine why the Columbine High School shootings took place in April of 1999. His daughter, Rachel Scott, was one of the students killed.

"Since the dawn of creation, there has been both good and evil in the hearts of men and women. We all contain the seeds of kindness or the seeds of violence. The death of my wonderful daughter, Rachel Joy Scott, and the deaths of that heroic teacher and the other eleven children who died must not be in vain. Their blood cries out for answers."

"The first recorded act of violence was when Cain slew his brother Abel out in the field. The villain was not the club he used. Neither was it the National Club Association. The true killer was Cain, and the reason for the murder could only be found in Cain's heart."

"In the days that followed the Columbine tragedy, I was amazed at how quickly fingers began to be pointed at groups such as the NRA. I am not a member of the NRA. I am not a hunter. I do not even own a gun. I am not here to represent or defend the NRA - because I do not believe that they are responsible for my daughter's death. Therefore, I do not believe that they need to be defended. If I believed they had anything to do with Rachel's murder, I would be their strongest opponent. I am here today to declare that Columbine was not just a tragedy-it was a Spiritual event that should be forcing us to look at where the real blame lies! Much of the blame lies here with Congress. Much of the blame lies behind the pointing fingers of the accusers themselves. I wrote a poem just four nights ago that expresses my feelings best. It was written before I knew I would be speaking here today."

"Your laws ignore our deepest needs; your words
are empty air.
You have stripped away our heritage, you have
outlawed simple prayer.
Now gunshots fill our classrooms, and precious
children die.
You seek for answers everywhere, and ask the
question "Why?"
You regulate restrictive laws, through legislative
creed
And yet you fail to understand, that God is what we
need!"

"Men and women are three-part beings. We all consist of body, soul, and Spirit. When we refuse to acknowledge a third part of our make-up, we create a void that allows evil, prejudice, and hatred to rush in and wreak havoc. Spiritual presences were present within our educational systems for <u>most</u> of our nation's history. Many of our major colleges began as theological seminaries. That is a historical fact. What has happened to us as a nation? We have refused to honor God, and in so doing, we open the doors to hatred and violence. And when something as terrible as Columbine's tragedy occurs -- politicians immediately look for a scapegoat, such as the NRA. They immediately seek to pass more restrictive laws that continue to erode our personal and private liberties. We do not need more restrictive laws. Metal detectors would not have stopped Eric and Dylan. Gun laws can not stop someone who spends months planning this type of massacre. The real villain lies within our hearts."

"As my son Craig lay under that table in the school library and saw his two friends murdered before his very eyes. <u>He did not hesitate to pray in school</u>. I defy any law or politician to deny him that right! I challenge every young person in America and around the world to realize that on April 20, 1999, at Columbine High School, <u>prayer was brought back to our schools</u>. Do not let the many prayers offered by those students be in vain. Dare to move into the new millennium with a sacred disregard for legislation that violates your God-given right to communicate with Him. To those who would point your finger at the NRA - I give you a sincere challenge. Dare to examine your own heart before casting the first stone! My daughter's death will not be in vain! The young people of this country will not allow that to happen!"

—☼—

Take Responsibility

My intent in presenting this very poignant message from a grieving father is not to change anyone's opinion about guns or organizations that are for or against the right to own guns. That is not the point of the story. I believe that the story's point was, and I know that my intent in repeating it is to demonstrate the necessity to take responsibility for our actions rather than looking for a scapegoat like Adam and Eve did. This story also points out that God created us with a need for Him in our lives, and when we deny that need, terrible things happen.

What are the things in your life that suffer from your lack of consistency? List these problems in your journal, and then elaborate on your plan to change these problems. Pray about those plans and note the changes whenever God tells you to modify any of your solutions. If you allow God's consistent power to control your life, you can trust that God will provide a better life for you than you could ever have imagined for yourself. Believe God loves you, let His unconditional and unlimited love work through you, and claim His promises for yourself. Live life and live it abundantly according to God's plan. Search diligently and fervently pray until you know what God's plan is for you. Have the faith that you can be all God wants you to be, which brings us to Chapter 8.

Discussion:

1. Have you ever doubted the consistency of God? _____

2. Do you think God has changed? _____

   a. Why do you think that? _____

   _____

   _____

   _____

3. Do you think the outcome of Adam & Eve's disobedience would have been different if they would have accepted responsibility for their actions? _____

4. How might it have been different? _____

   _____

   _____

   _____

5. . Think of the one thing in your life that best demonstrates God's consistency or the appearance of inconsistency. _____

   _____

   _____

   _____

Call to Action:

1. What are the things in your life that suffer from your lack of consistency? List these problems in your journal, and then elaborate on how you plan to change these problems.

2. Pray about your plans, then write down any changes to these plans that God reveals to you in these prayers.

Reading List, Faith:

Hebrews 11:1-40   Mark 11:20-25
Matthew 17:14-20   John 6:22-40
Acts 6:1-8:3   Acts 9:1-19
James 2:1-26

Additional Scripture references:

_____

_____

Chapter 8, Faith

Now faith is the assurance of things hoped for, the conviction of things not seen. Indeed, by faith our ancestors received approval. By faith we understand that the worlds were prepared by the word of God, so that what is seen was made from things that are not visible.... And without faith, it is impossible to please God, for whoever would approach him must believe that he exists and that he rewards those who seek him (Heb 11:1-3, 6).

The entire eleventh chapter of Hebrews is about faith. It starts by defining faith, as quoted above in verse 1, and then gives many examples from the Old Testament. These examples all have one thing in common. Something that is not obvious or provable by typical human methods. As stated in the sixth verse. Even, and maybe especially, pleasing God requires faith because we must first believe He exists before we can please Him.

Faith is the foundation of all aspects of our relationship with God. And when we fail at anything that is God's work, it is due to our lack of faith! The Gospel of Mark records the following statement by Christ in response to a comment by Peter about a withered fig tree.

Jesus answered them, "Have faith in God. Truly I tell you, if you say to this mountain, 'Be taken up and thrown into the sea,' and if you do not doubt in your heart, but believe that what you say will come to pass, it will be done for you. So I tell you, whatever you ask for in prayer, believe that you have received it, and it will be yours. Whenever you stand praying, forgive, if you have anything against anyone; so that your Father in heaven may also forgive you your trespasses" (Mark 11:22-25).

Faith is Empowerment

Christ commands us to "Have faith in God." He tells us that there is no limit to what we can do in God's name if we have faith! In other words, when we fail at anything that is truly God's work, it is due to our lack of faith. As stated, this seems to be very harsh. It almost appears that we may be to blame if we are unsuccessful when trying to do God's work! Well, welcome to the real world. We do have responsibilities. First, do not forget verse 25 of the quote above: we must forgive anyone that we have a grievance against before we are able to accept the forgiveness that God is offering us. Second, God actually expects us to listen to what He tells us and to trust in His power to work in and through our lives. The problem comes when we confuse the idea of having faith in God with sitting and doing nothing. God is telling us is that if we trust Him and have faith, we can do more. Faith <u>is not the replacement</u> for our actions; <u>it is the empowerment</u> of our actions. Faith is believing that God will give us direction on what He wants us to do, the patience to wait for His guidance, and the power to do what He tells us when we have received His direction. The following story about a little girl and her father shows something about faith.

The Necklace

The cheerful little girl with bouncy golden curls was almost five. Waiting with her mother at the checkout stand, she saw them, a circle of glistening white pearls in a pink foil box.

"Oh, Mommy, please, Mommy. Can I have them? Please, Mommy, please?"

Quickly the mother checked the back of the little foil box and then looked back into the pleading blue eyes of her little girl's upturned face.

"A dollar ninety-five, that's almost $2.00. If you really want them, I will think of some extra chores for you, and in no time, you can save enough money to buy them for yourself. Your birthday's only a week away, and you might get another crisp dollar bill from Grandma."

As soon as Jenny got home, she emptied her penny bank and counted out 17 pennies. After dinner, she did more than her share of chores, and she went to the neighbor and asked Mrs. McJames if she could pick dandelions for ten cents. On her birthday, Grandma did give her another new dollar bill, and at last, she had enough money to buy the necklace.

Jenny loved her pearls. They made her feel dressed up and grown-up. She wore them everywhere, Sunday school, kindergarten, even to bed. The only time she took them off was when she went swimming or had a bubble bath. Her mother said that if they got wet, they might turn her neck green.

Jenny had a very loving daddy, and every night when she was ready for bed, he would stop whatever he was doing and come upstairs to read her a story. One night as he finished the story, he asked Jenny, "Do you love me?"

"Oh yes, Daddy. You know that I love you."

"Then give me your pearls."

"Oh, daddy, not my pearls, but you can have Princess, the white horse from my collection, the one with the pink tail. Remember Daddy? The one you gave me. She's my very favorite."

"That's okay, Honey. Daddy loves you. Good night." And he brushed her cheek with a kiss.

About a week later, after the storytime, Jenny's daddy asked again, "Do you love me?"

"Daddy, you know I love you."

"Then give me your pearls."

"Oh, Daddy, not my pearls, but you can have my baby doll. The brand new one I got for my birthday. She is beautiful, and you can have the yellow blanket that matches her sleeper."

"That's okay. Sleep well. God bless you, little one. Daddy loves you."

And as always, he brushed her cheek with a gentle kiss.

A few nights later, when her daddy came in, Jenny was sitting on her bed with her legs crossed Indian style. As he came close, he noticed her chin was trembling, and one silent tear rolled down her cheek.

"What is it, Jenny? What's the matter?"

Jenny did not say anything but lifted her little hand up to her daddy. When she opened it, there was her little pearl necklace. With a little quiver, she finally said, "Here, Daddy, this is for you."

With tears gathering in his own eyes, Jenny's daddy reached out with one hand to take the dime-store necklace, and with the other hand, he reached into his pocket, pulled out a blue velvet case with a strand of genuine pearls, and gave them to Jenny. He had them all the time. He was just waiting for her to give up the imitation pearls so he could give her the genuine treasure.

God Must be First

Does this sound a little harsh—a father asking his little girl if she loved him and then asking her to give up her very favorite thing? Does this story sound as if the father's love was conditional? No, the father always assured Jenny that he loved her, even though she had not complied with his request. The story, of course, is an analogy. The little girl represents a person who is immature in their relationship with God. The person the story is talking about loves God and is aware of God's love. She may even realize that God's love is unconditional and unlimited. However, this is not enough. There is something in her life that is more important than her relationship with God. Belief in God, believing that God is all-powerful, knowing He is the creator—none of these is enough. For us to be able to accept God's gift of Faith, we must go right back to where this book started. Chapter 1 showed us that God's love for us is so great that he gave His son to die for our sins. If we are to receive all of God's gifts, our love of Him must be so great that we will allow nothing on this earth to come between God and ourselves. We must put God first. Our chins may quiver a little as we give up the earthly treasures that keep us from a complete relationship with God—but our faith will grow each time we give the costume treasures to God and allow Him to provide us with the genuine treasure in return.

Unbelieving and Perverse

Chapters 17 of both Matthew and Luke relate some additional stories about faith. These stores show us what happens when our faith is inadequate. They also show what amazing power that we have to do God's work when we have faith. Chapter 17 of Matthew tells us the disciples responded to the request of a man whose son was having seizures. They tried to heal him but, they were not effective. The man then sees Christ and tells him three things. First, he relates his son's problem. Second, he tells Christ that he has already asked the disciples to heal his son. Lastly, he tells Christ that the disciples tried to heal his son, but they were unsuccessful. At this point, it seems that Christ is a little irritated with the disciples. He calls them unbelieving and perverse, and then He asks them a rhetorical question: *"How long shall I stay with you? How long shall I put up with you?"* Then He heals the boy.

Too Little Faith

The disciples are upset with themselves. They do not understand why Christ could heal the boy, but they could not. They had started to believe that they had the power to do almost anything, but now the disciples were ineffective, and they did not understand why. After everyone but the disciples has left, leaving them alone with Christ, they ask Him why they could not heal the boy. From the Gospel of Matthew,

> *Then the disciples came to Jesus in private and asked, "Why couldn't we drive it out?" He replied, "Because you have so little faith. I tell you the truth, if you have faith as small as a mustard seed, you can say to this mountain, 'Move from here to there' and it will move. Nothing will be impossible for you."*
> (Matt. 17:19-20, NIV).

In Luke, the words are a bit different.

> *The apostles said to the Lord, "Increase our faith!" He replied, "If you have faith as small as a mustard seed, you can say to this mulberry tree, 'Be uprooted and planted in the sea,' and it will obey you"* (Luke 17:5-6, NIV).

Considering the topic and how both are talking about the "Faith of a mustard seed," the two passages from Matthew and Luke are likely the same lesson by Christ to His disciples. If we look at them together, the request made to Christ by the disciples recorded in Luke 17:5 makes a lot more sense. Matthew tells us that the disciples have failed in an attempt to heal a boy. The father then brings him to Christ, who heals the boy and tells the disciples that they do not have enough faith or they could have healed the boy. Luke relates that the disciples ask Christ to increase their faith. The fact that the disciples ask Christ to increase their faith implies two things. First, they cannot do this on their own. The disciples did not ask Christ what they had to do to increase their faith. They seem to know that they cannot just concentrate harder, or just work harder, or study more, and expect to have more faith. Faith is not something that originates within man. Similarly, we cannot increase our faith by our efforts. The second implication is that Christ will give them more faith. In other words, faith is a gift from God.

Faith is a Gift

John Chapter 6 is also supportive of the idea that faith is a gift from God.

> *All that the Father gives me will come to me, and whoever comes to me I will never drive away. For I have come down from heaven not to do my will but to do the will of him who sent me. And this is the will of him who sent me, that I shall lose none of all that he has given me, but raise them up at the last day. For my Father's will is that everyone who looks to the Son and believes in him shall have eternal life, and I will raise him up at the last day* (John 6:37-40, NIV).

In this passage, Christ is talking about salvation, and we know from many of Paul's writings that faith is the requirement to receive salvation. As Christ is stating that "the Father" (God) is "giving" persons to Christ to be saved, we can conclude from this verse of scripture also that faith is a gift from God.

Can You Accept the Gift?

The writers of the New Testament frequently couple faith with repentance. It is not that God withholds His gift of faith until we repent; it is that we are <u>not able to accept</u> that gift or any other of God's gifts until we meet the conditions of each gift. For the gift of faith, we are required to repent. As repentance requires acceptance of responsibility for one's actions, the gift of faith is like God's gift of consistency. For us to accept any of God's gifts, we must first take responsibility for our actions. Unless you pry your heart from the passing pleasures of sin, you will never see God.

How will our lives change when we accept God's gift of faith in our lives? What will be different that those around us can see? Paul tells us that it is by our faith that we find salvation. James tells us that when he sees a change in our lives, that is evidence of our faith. Paul certainly is a primary authority on and about faith in New Testament times. We need to look into his background to get an idea of where his thoughts about faith originate.

The person we know as the Apostle Paul is introduced as Saul in the seventh chapter of Acts. It is the story about the stoning of Stephen.

> But Stephen, full of the Holy Spirit, looked up to heaven and saw the glory of God, and Jesus standing at the right hand of God. "Look," he said, "I see heaven open and the Son of Man standing at the right hand of God." At this they covered their ears and, yelling at the top of their voices, they all

rushed at him, dragged him out of the city and begin to stone him. Meanwhile, the witnesses laid their clothes at the feet of a young man named Saul. While they were stoning him, Stephen prayed, "Lord Jesus, receive my spirit." Then he fell on his knees and cried out, "Lord, do not hold this sin against them." When he had said this, he fell asleep. And Saul was there, giving approval to his death. On that day a great persecution broke out against the church at Jerusalem, and all except the apostles were scattered throughout Judea and Samaria. Godly men buried Stephen and mourned deeply for him. But Saul began to destroy the church. Going from house to house, he dragged off men and women and put them in prison (Acts 7:55-8:3, NIV).

Saul then goes to the high priest and obtains letters to the synagogues in Damascus so that if he found any there that belonged to "The Way," he could arrest them and take them back to Jerusalem. Chapter 9 of Acts relates the experience of Saul when he was on the road to Damascus. In this experience, Christ tells Saul that he is God's chosen instrument to carry the name of Christ to the Gentiles, their kings, and all of Israel. Saul's personal experience on the road and for the next few days in Damascus was what he, now renamed to Paul, then preached to the Gentiles. Repent, receive forgiveness for your sins, and be sanctified by faith. This experience of Paul is also evidence that faith is a gift from God. Later, in the third chapter of Romans, Paul is telling the Romans the same thing.

For we maintain that a man is justified by faith apart from observing the law
(Rom. 3:28, NIV).

The words are different, but the message Paul is telling us is the same. Whether you talk about being *"sanctified by faith"* or *"justified by faith,"* the meaning is the same. It is through our faith, which is a gift from God, that we find salvation. Being sure of our salvation is another evidence of our having accepted the gift of God's faith.

Faith and Deeds

Looking at what James has to say about faith:

> *But someone will say, "You have faith; I have deeds." Show me your faith without deeds, and I will show you my faith by what I do. You believe that there is one God. Good! Even the demons believe that--and shudder* (James 2:18-19, NIV).

At first glance, this scripture and the scripture in Acts and the positions of Paul and James presented elsewhere in the Bible; seem to be at odds. Maybe so, but only on the surface, if you read all of the letters of Paul, you can't escape the fact that he believes that true faith in God will result in not wanting to sin and in trying to do God's will. James is saying this same thing. Faith without deeds is dead. There is no way you can truly accept the gift of faith from God and look only for your personal salvation. Both James and Paul tell us that true faith will not allow us to ignore other people's needs. The evidence of our faith is that our lives are changed. God changes our lives in a way that will show those around us we have accepted God's gift of faith.

Even though faith is a gift from God, we must repent and do our best to follow the will of God if we are to accept His gift of faith. Faith is the requirement for our salvation. We evidence the amount and quality of our faith in all that we do, especially in our relationships with all of God's children. Again, we find ourselves back to God's greatest gift, as related in John 3:16. Christ and faith in Him are the sources of our salvation and the basis of the change in our lives from following our natural human tendencies to following God's plan. This gift of faith is one of the promises offered by God that is ours to accept.

Repent – Believe – Accept

What are you doing to accept this gift of faith from God? Are you letting this gift change the way that you live your life? Repent, believe, and accept God's gift of salvation through His gift of faith! Seek to understand God's saving justice in relationships with other people. What are your pieces of costume jewelry that God is waiting to replace in your life? What do you need to give up for your acceptance of God's gift of faith to be complete? Write it down, put the piece of paper in your hand, and offer it to God. You will be amazed at what He has in His hand, just waiting for you to accept it.

Discussion:

1. Do you believe that faith is a gift or that faith is what you must already have to receive any of God's gifts? __

   _____

2. What happened between the time of the Gospels, when the disciples showed such a lack of faith, and later in the book of Acts? _____

   _____

   _____

3. If faith is a gift, what, if anything, can we do to increase our faith? _____

   _____

   _____

4. What are you doing to accept this gift of faith from God? _____

   _____

   _____

5. Are you letting this gift change the way that you live your life? _____

6. Define or discuss **your** faith and how it works in your life. _____

   _____

   _____

   _____

7. What in your life is the best evidence of your faith? ___

   _____

   _____

   _____

Call to Action:

1. Are you letting this gift change the way that you live your life? Repent, believe, and accept God's gift of salvation through His gift of faith!

2. Seek to understand God's saving justice in relationships with other people.

3. Write down in your journal what your pieces of costume jewelry are that God is waiting to replace in your life. What do you need to give up for your acceptance of God's gift of faith to be complete? Write it down, put the piece of paper in your hand, and offer it to God. You will be amazed at what He has in His hand, just waiting for you to accept it. Note in your journal what you have offered to God and His response.

Reading List, God's Saving Justice:

Romans 3:1-31   Luke 15:11-32
Matthew 20:1-16   John 15:1-17
1 John 3:11-24   James 1:19-27
John 10: 7-18

Additional Scripture references:

_____

_____

Chapter 9, God's Saving Justice

*for all have sinned and fall short of the glory
of God* (Rom. 3:23b, NIV).

That sounds like bad news. No exceptions, we have
all sinned, and we are all less than what God has
planned for us.

Yes, I used the same scripture in the chapter on grace,
and there certainly is a relationship between God's grace and
God's Saving Justice. However, they are not the same. So, let
me continue with Romans 3:23. Looking at this one verse by
itself is an excellent example of why you need to read more
than just one verse at a time to get the correct meaning of the
Bible. Let us read the three before and three after and then look
again for the message—maybe something about God's saving
justice?

> *Therefore no one will be declared righteous in
> his sight by observing the law; rather, through the
> law we become conscious of sin. But now a
> righteousness from God, apart from law, has been
> made known, to which the Law and the Prophets
> testify. This righteousness from God comes through
> faith in Jesus Christ to all who believe. There is no
> difference, for all have sinned and fall short of the
> glory of God, and are justified freely by his grace
> through the redemption that came by Christ Jesus.
> God presented him as a sacrifice of atonement,*

115

through faith in his blood. He did this to demonstrate his justice, because in his forbearance he had left the sins committed beforehand unpunished--he did it to demonstrate his justice at the present time, so as to be just and the one who justifies those who have faith in Jesus (Rom. 3:20-26, NIV).

Why, Because of God's Sense of Justice

First, we see why Paul made the statement. He is telling the Romans that it does not make any difference whether they are Jews or Gentiles. The law has served to make the Jews conscious of sin but has never allowed God to declare them righteous. Therefore, we are all starting from the same sinful condition, and God's gift of righteousness is available through faith in Jesus Christ, regardless of our heritage, to all who believe in Him. It does not make any difference because, Jew or Gentile, we all have sinned and need God's gift of righteousness. Moreover, His gift is available to all who believe in Christ Jesus. Why did God do this? Why is this gift available to everyone? It is available because of God's sense of justice. God is not concerned about our past; He has forgiven everyone and is offering the gift of His saving justice to all who believe. He has even held off His judgment for all those sins committed before Christ. So now you can see why the same verses of scripture are used both in the discussion on God's "Grace" and in the discussion on "God's Saving Justice." God's grace is the source of our redemption, but it is God's Saving Justice, His sense of justice, that is the reason that He has made His grace available to us.

Unlimited Resources, No One Deserves

We frequently complain about God's sense of justice because we do not understand God's compassion for us or His unlimited resources to provide for us. So we say, "It's not fair!" We make this statement when we perceive that someone we have determined is "unworthy" receives benefits in life that we think should have been ours, or at least not theirs. This concept of fairness by human standards is so ingrained in our society that a "troubleshooter" on a television station in Southern California uses this expression after describing the problem, declaring in a very determined voice: "It's not fair!"

In the Bible, this is the story of the older brother of the prodigal son found in Luke 15:11-32. The older brother has not recognized the gifts he has always received by doing his father's will. The older brother is jealous of what the father is doing for his ungrateful son, who squandered his inheritance and now has come back wanting his father to take care of him. You can almost hear the older brother saying, "It's not fair!" I am sure that the older brother does not believe that the prodigal son has fully repented. Moreover, he probably thinks he will be required to share part of his inheritance with the returning brother, even though he has already squandered half of his father's wealth. A contrast of what the older brother is thinking compared to what the father knows might look like this:

The Older Brother *Thinks*	The Father *Knows*
He has not earned a celebration	It is a gift of my love
He has denied you	He has come back
He is just using you	I accept him
He will want part of <u>my</u> inheritance	There is no limit to what I have to give
I stayed and obeyed	My love has surrounded you
I earned my inheritance	No one can earn salvation
He is getting special treatment	Everyone gets special treatment
It is not fair!	It is my saving justice!

Many times when we study the story of the Prodigal son, we stop at the end of verse 24, *"And they began to celebrate."* That is because the story of the Prodigal son is such a marvelous story. We see God with His open arms, ready to accept us whenever we are ready, regardless of how we have squandered His gifts to us. However, this is not the end of the story or the lesson! There are many times in our lives that we are more like the older brother. The father's conversation with him is the message we need to hear. We want our sense of justice in the world, not God's Saving Justice. We seem to feel that God is limited in His resources and that if someone else gets "more than they deserve" then, we will receive "less than we deserve." Two erroneous assumptions lead to these thoughts. First, there is no limit to God's resources. Relative to our understanding, every one of us can receive 100% of God's gifts, and He will never run out. Second, no one has deserved, or will ever deserve, even a tiny fraction of the gifts that God is waiting to provide for us if we will just accept them in our lives.

Based on the number of times that Christ talked about our misunderstanding of His saving justice, we can conclude that it was as prevalent a problem in that time as we know it is now. We can find another example of our sense of justice compared to God's justice in Matthew 20:1-16, the story of the laborers in the vineyard. Those workers that came at the start of the day received what they considered fair pay for a day's work. Their problem was that they could not accept others only working for a half-day and receiving a full day's payment. To compound matters for the full-day workers' sense of justice, another group worked for only one hour and still received a full day's pay. In the full-day worker's view, that was not fair. Either those who had worked the entire day needed to receive more compensation, or the part-day workers should have received less pay. Otherwise, the landowner was not fair.

Again, we are limiting our understanding of God and the extent of His resources. We are acting as if it is a penalty to have spent more of our lives with God. Moreover, we are implying that a person who only spends a few days or even a few moments with God has gotten away with something we were not allowed to do.

He First Loved Us

How misguided our education has been relative to our relationship with God. Do we worship a vindictive, manipulating God? Were we asleep throughout the entire New Testament? Don't we remember the words in John 3:16?

In Chapter 15 of the Gospel of John, Christ said,

> *This is my commandment, that you love one another, as I have loved you* (John 15:12).

Then in 1 John, we read:

> *This is how we know what love is: Jesus Christ laid down his life for us. And we ought to lay down our lives for our brothers* (1 John 3:16).

He first loved us. God loved us so much that He sacrificed His only son so that we could spend eternity with Him. Christ's sacrifice is the definition of love and the source of the love we should have for one another. However, John has more to say. He follows this definition of love by an admonishment that we must follow what Christ did for us. Moreover, we must be willing to lay down our life for another of God's children.

As children, we sang "Jesus Loves Me." When did we stop believing that? Perhaps we believe it, but we just do not think that God is involved in our lives. The truth is that God is as involved as we will let Him be! We are in control of how involved God is in our lives. He has given us free will. Somehow, we have determined that when we use our free will to go against God's will, we have gotten away with something and are somehow better off.

Less Than We Could Be

In reality, we have cheated ourselves. When we do something we know is against God's will, we try to hide from Him. We know we cannot hide from God. We just leave ourselves with another portion of our life that is less pleasant and less productive than it could have been. Also, while we are hiding, we cannot hear and accept what God is trying to do in our lives. There is another way to look at our strange sense of justice. If it is our idea—that we are ahead and will enjoy life more—when we live our earthly lives outside of the presence of God, why would we want to spend the time after our temporal death in the presence of God? If we are not comfortable with God now, then "being saved" at the last moment of our lives and spending the rest of eternity with God would be punishment. If we want to spend eternity with God, we need to remember that eternity has already started. Eternity not only includes the future, but it also includes the present.

Anger Can Separate Us from God

At the end of the first chapter of James, he specifically mentions anger as one of the emotions that can separate us from God's Saving Justice. Later, James expands his list to all impurities and remnants of evil. James tells us that any aspect of our life where we are not living within God's will can keep us from accepting God's Saving Justice.

> *My dear brothers, take note of this: Everyone should be quick to listen, slow to speak and slow to become angry, for man's anger does not bring about the righteous life that God desires. Therefore, get rid of all moral filth and the evil that is so prevalent and humbly accept the word planted in you, which can save you* (James 1:19-21, NIV).

"*...man's anger does not bring about the righteous life that God desires.*" Alternatively, as it is presented in the New Jerusalem Bible, "*God's saving justice is not served by human anger.*" The righteous life is for everyone whenever we are ready to accept it. It makes no difference—as far as the availability of God's saving justice—whether we spend our entire life serving God, or we spend only the last few seconds of our life confessing our sins and asking for His saving justice. I repeat, His saving justice is there for all whenever we are ready to accept it! That is certainly not to say that God does not care how we live our lives. He wants us to follow His will so that we: *"may have life, and have it abundantly."* (John 10:10b) God is waiting while we are wasting what should be a wonderful life with Him. We delay seeking to do His will and accepting God's saving justice, all the time thinking that we have come out ahead. How wrong we are, and how much it costs us and those with whom we associate.

How Do You Respond?

Our anger is probably one of the most frequent transgressions that separate us from God. How do you respond when someone cuts in front of you in a long line, or cuts you off on the road, or has 20 items in the "10 items or less" checkout line? Is your first response one of anger and your first thought of how to get even? Are you convinced that you must "educate" the transgressor of the error of their way? That is frequently my response. This type of anger response is habitual; I may be fighting it for the rest of my life. It has been a long time since I tried to return the favor when someone cut me off on the road, but I still think about it. Yet, there are so many negative aspects of this type of response and absolutely nothing positive. First, it is dangerous. You may rationalize that you need to educate this misguided person so that they will not do it again. You know that will not work. You are exposing yourself and anyone else on the road to additional danger through your actions. Second, instead of allowing your body to recover from the rise in blood pressure from the initial scare that the person would hit you, you continue to pump the adrenaline by trying to cut them off. Ultimately, the more we respond in anger to situations around us that do not fit our sense of justice, the more we encourage that action in others. That is particularly true if we have children in our car who learn a lot more from our actions than from what we tell them we believe. Our aggressive response to a situation we disapprove of will teach those around us that this is the appropriate response when angry with someone.

On the other hand, the following story shows how extraordinary the result can be when we look at life with God's sense of justice. We must put aside a part of our competitive emphasis, stop looking at how we view what is fair and let God work through our actions.

Where is God's Plan

At a fundraising dinner for a school that serves learning-disabled children, the father of one of the school's students delivered a speech that would never be forgotten by those that attended.

After extolling the school and its dedicated staff, he made a statement of belief followed by a question of God's Justice. "Everything God does is done with perfection. Yet, my son Shay cannot learn things as other children do. He cannot understand things as other children do. Where is God's plan reflected in my son?"

The audience was stilled by the query. The father continued. "I believe that when God brings a child like Shay into the world, an opportunity to realize the Divine Plan presents itself, and it comes in the way people treat that child." Then, he told the following story:

Shay and his father had walked past a park where some boys Shay knew were playing baseball. Shay asked, "Do you think they will let me play?" Shay's father knew that the boys would not want him on their team. But the father understood that if his son were allowed to play, it would give him a much-needed sense of belonging. Shay's father approached one of the boys on the field and asked if Shay could play. The boy looked around for guidance from his teammates. Getting none, he took matters into his own hands and said, "We are losing by six runs, and the game is in the eighth inning. I guess he can be on our team, and we'll try to put him up to bat in the ninth inning." In the bottom of the eighth inning, Shay's team scored a few runs but was still behind by three. At the top of the ninth inning, Shay put on a glove and played in the outfield. Although no hits came his way, he was obviously ecstatic just to be on the field, grinning from ear to ear as his father waved to him from the stands. In the bottom of the ninth inning, Shay's team scored again. Now, with two outs and the bases loaded, the potential winning run was on base. Shay was scheduled to be the next at-bat. Would the team let Shay bat and give away their chance to win the game? Surprisingly, Shay was given the bat. Everyone knew that a hit was all but impossible because Shay did not even know how to hold the bat properly, much less connect with the ball. However, as Shay stepped up to the plate, the pitcher moved a few steps to lob the ball in softly so Shay could at least be able to make contact. The first pitch came, and Shay swung clumsily and missed. The pitcher again took a few steps forward to toss the ball softly toward Shay. As the pitch came in, Shay swung at the ball and hit a slow ground ball to the pitcher. The pitcher picked up the soft grounder and could easily have thrown the ball to the first baseman. Shay would have been out, and that would have ended the game. Instead, the pitcher took the ball and threw it on a high arc to right field, far beyond the reach of the first baseman. Everyone started yelling, "Shay, run to first, run to first." Never in his life had Shay ever made it to first base. He scampered down the baseline, wide-eyed and startled. Everyone yelled, "Run to second, run to second!" By the time Shay was rounding first base, the right fielder had the ball. He could have thrown the ball to the second baseman for a tag. However, the right fielder understood the pitcher's intentions, so he threw the ball high and far over the third baseman's head. Shay ran towards second base as the runners ahead of him deliriously circled the bases towards home. As Shay reached second base, the opposing shortstop ran to him, turned him in the direction of third base, and shouted, "Run to third!" As Shay rounded third, the boys from both teams were screaming, "Shay Run home!" Shay ran home, stepped on home plate, and was cheered as the hero for hitting a "grand slam" and winning the game for his team. "That day," said the father softly with tears now rolling down his face, "the boys from both teams helped bring a piece of the Divine Plan into this world."

This story has circulated on the internet and in email for years. As I have not been able to determine the source of this story, I do not know for sure that it is true. However, it illustrates how God can work through us if we look at life through His sense of justice rather than our feelings of what is fair. Therefore, I choose to believe that it is true.

Strive for God's Inner Peace

Consider the difference in your life, whether you react to life's situations insisting everyone follow your sense of fairness or, with compassion like the kids in the story about Shay. Do you want to live your life spending your energy in an angry response to the actions of others, or do you desire to receive the power that comes from being compassionate and trying to see how God views each situation? Moreover, if that difference is not sufficient to change your ways, don't you have enough other things in your life separating you from a perfect relationship with God without adding another every time something happens that does not suit your sense of justice? I certainly do. Practice counting to ten, taking a deep breath, and relaxing the next time you find yourself in a situation that angers you. That should give the transgressor time to get out of your sight and time for you to thank God for saving you from yourself. On the other hand, maybe all you need to do is let the child in you see each situation with compassion and God's sense of justice. Either way, it will help you feel God's inner peace in your life.

Discussion:

1. How is your sense of justice different than what the scripture tells us about God's sense of justice? _____

   _____

   _____

2. Do you believe that there are any persons that God either cannot or will not forgive? _____

3. List some persons in your life that "your sense of justice" tells you are unworthy of God's Saving Grace.

   _____

   _____

4. What can you do to bring "your sense of justice" in line with what the scripture tells us is God's sense of justice? _____

   _____

   _____

   _____

5. Do you think it was fair to the players on the other team to let Shay's team win even though they did not earn it? Explain. _____

   _____

   _____

   _____

Call to Action:

1. Practice counting to ten, taking a deep breath and relaxing the next time you find yourself in a situation that tries your sense of justice.

2. Memorize a Bible verse like Matthew 5:45 and repeat it when another person's actions test your understanding of God's sense of justice.

3. Look for situations where you can help someone else receive God's saving grace.

4. Enjoy your sense of God's inner peace returning in your life.

5. Record your successes in your journal.

Reading List, Peace:

Philippians 4:2-9   John 14:1-31
Matthew 5:43-48   Matthew 10:1-42
Mark 5:25-34   James 1:1-8

Additional Scripture references:

_____

_____

Chapter 10, Peace

Do we understand what "the peace of God" means? In Philippians, we read:

> *Do not worry about anything, but in everything by prayer and supplication with thanksgiving let your requests be made known to God. And the <u>peace of God, which surpasses all understanding</u>, will guard your hearts and your minds in Christ Jesus* (Phil. 4:6-7).

This scripture does not explain to us what the peace of God is, but it does tell us something about what we need to do to receive it. First, we are not to worry. Second, we are to make our requests known to God—through prayer and supplication with thanksgiving. The scripture also tells us that the peace of God is beyond anything we can understand. It is so magnificent it is beyond our imagination! The book of John gives us another clue.

> *Peace I leave with you; my peace I give you. I do not give to you as the world gives. Do not let your hearts be troubled and do not be afraid.* (John 14:27, NIV).

Not What the World Understands

The world does not understand the kind of peace that is a gift from God. We cannot create it by ourselves; we can only accept it as a gift from God. In John, Christ also tells us that if we accept His peace, we do not need to be afraid, and we do not need to be concerned or worried. Christ tells the disciples that He is going away but that the Holy Spirit will come and give them peace in their hearts.

The following is an excerpt from a poem titled "Mama, Did You Know?" written by David L. Weatherford to his mother. The first paragraph tells why he wrote the poem, and the rest is one section of the poem about inner peace.

Mama, Did You Know?

I believe a mother's love is proof of a Higher Power, for something so pure and beautiful could only come from the grace of God. I have been so sweetly blessed with a magnificent mother who I could never possibly deserve. She is the great love of my life. She is very ill now, and it hurts my heart like no other pain I have ever known. This poem is my attempt to describe the beauty of my mother and my undying devotion to her. It is a daunting task to express such large and powerful feelings, and certainly, any words I may put together will be woefully inadequate to capture the depth, breadth, and wonder of her life and the glorious way she has filled the role of mother. In taking on this challenge, I am not unlike the man who stood on the mountaintop with a small brush, imagining he could paint the endless sky. Nevertheless, here is my effort to create a tribute to my beloved mother and all she means to me.

Mama, did you know that one of my major life goals has been to please you? There were times in my young life when I simply lacked direction and motivation. I didn't know who I was or where I was going. But I always made the effort to be productive and forward-moving, if only because I knew that would make you proud. When I was lost, or without goals, I simply did what I thought you might want me to do. And you know what, mama -- that always kept me on a pretty good path.

Did you know that when I was a child you were the center of my universe? You were the sun, the light, the answer – you were God to me before I knew Him. Of course, you taught me to worship the one true God, and He became the Center of Everything. But, mama, you will forever remain in the center of my heart.

Did you know that from childhood to adulthood, I have admired a wondrous gift you possess –that amazing sense of calm deep within you? It gives you a quiet strength, a sense of certainty, a will that never wavers, a profound truth. I have come to understand that this inner well of peace derives from your indomitable faith in the Lord. So I strive to find that for myself.

Dear God, if I could make a wish for the world, it would be that every child might have a mother like mine. If they did, everyone would grow up beautifully loved, emotionally nourished, and fully prepared to share the faith, joy, and hope that was nurtured in their hearts.

David L. Weatherford

—☼—

Responsible for Our Actions

Part of this gift of peace from God is to know what we are responsible for and what we are not. We are not responsible for correcting other people's mistakes. As I said in the previous chapter, if someone cuts you off while you are driving, it is not your responsibility to make sure that they know that this is not appropriate driving etiquette. You are only responsible for ensuring that you are following the driving rules.

Our responsibility is for our actions. If we insist on trying to take the responsibility to educate others as to the nature of their offense, the result will be to minimize the sense of God's peace in our own life. It is not a good result by itself, but it is even worse when you consider that the process we would use to educate the offender will probably expose others and ourselves to dangers as bad as, or worse than, the one we feel we need to correct. While we are thinking about all the reasons we should correct someone's mistake, we imagine that we will feel a sense of justification when we have made the offender aware of the error of his way.

Sense of Guilt More Likely

What happens is our anger will build, and when we have completed our task, we are much more likely to feel a sense of guilt rather than a sense of justification. We certainly will not enhance our feeling of inner peace. On the other hand, if we take a deep breath to get over the initial shock and stop that surge of anger, then we can allow God's inner peace to take control and common sense to prevail. Then we can offer a prayer of thanksgiving that God has protected both the offender and ourselves. If these words sound a little like what you read in the previous chapter, it is because they are. Most times, when we insist on following our sense of justice rather than letting God's saving justice be in control, it is our sense of inner peace that suffers.

Another problem keeping us from accepting God's gift of peace is that God does not seem to discriminate on how He distributes His blessings. Persons we may feel are undeserving seem to receive as much as those who we think do deserve. As the Bible tells us, God makes the rain fall upon the just and the unjust! That is God's decision, not ours. It is not our job to determine who will receive the benefits of God's gifts any more than it is our job to correct the mistakes of others. The only thing that will happen when we start complaining about what others are receiving is to reduce our ability to accept God's gift of peace. Christ told us:

> *Love your enemies, bless them that curse you, do good to them that hate you, and pray for them which despitefully use you, and persecute you; That ye may be the children of your Father which is in heaven: for he maketh his sun to rise on the evil and on the good, and sendeth rain on the just and on the unjust.* (Matt. 5:44b-45, KJV).

Rather than feeling that we have received the short end of the stick or that others have received more than they deserved, we should be looking for ways to show our love for people in the way Christ has shown us. This action will enhance our ability to accept God's gifts but feeling sorry for ourselves or being jealous of another will at least inhibit, if not destroy, our sense of inner peace.

The Source of Real Peace

In addition to the driving example, many other areas can keep us from accepting the gift of God's peace. First, it *is not* our responsibility to correct or discipline anyone that we determine has invaded our space, stepped on our rights, or taken away our feeling of peace and calm. Second, we need to remember the source of real peace. Real peace is a gift from God and is within us. Others can temporarily disturb our sense of peace by their actions, but we are the only ones that can block it. We can refuse to accept this gift from God by our actions.

In the tenth chapter of the book of Matthew, Christ told us to withhold our peace from others in situations where we might be inclined to respond with anger. He also instructs the disciples and gives them a level of authority for healing. That is in preparation for them going out as missionaries.

> *If the house is worthy, let your peace come upon it; but if it is not worthy, let your peace return to you. If anyone will not welcome you or listen to your words, shake off the dust from your feet as you leave that house or town* (Matt. 10:13-14).

We must remember what kind of peace that Christ is talking about. He is talking about the peace that is a gift from God. As we read later in Matthew, this is not the peace of the world. The absence of war does not describe this peace. It is not necessarily the absence of physical or mental conflict. Let's read from Matthew Chapter 10,

> *Do not think that I have come to bring peace to the earth; I have not come to bring peace, but a sword. For I have come to set a man against his father, and a daughter against her mother, and a daughter-in-law against her mother-in-law; and one's foes will be members of one's own household* (Matt. 10:34-36).

The Peace of Knowing God

That sounds harsh, doesn't it? In this scripture, Christ is telling us that His peace is not the peace of the world. In fact, if you follow Him, you likely will not have the kind of peace that we expect. The peace that we can accept from God is an inner peace that tells us that nothing else matters when we know God and are in tune with God's plan for us. The book of Mark gives the following example of the peace that God gives us.

> *He said to her, "Daughter, your faith has made you well; go in peace, and be healed of your disease"* (Mark 5:34).

The source of this women's peace was not just an absence of her chronic illness. Her peace resulted from her confidence in the power of knowing what God could do in her life. As Christ said, her faith had made her well. This same faith had also allowed her to accept the gift of inner peace that came from knowing God was in control of her life.

God's Peace Equals Freedom

When we have accepted God's peace, we are free to live our lives according to God's will without worrying about how others try to influence us. We no longer have to worry about the actions of other people. We just have to take responsibility for our actions to continue to live with God's peace within us. When we stray from our state of inner peace and show our anger to others, we have but to confess to God, and He will restore our inner peace.

There are other emotions that we may have besides anger that can take away our inner peace. One of them is resentment, another is holding a grudge, and still another, is knowing that we have wronged one of God's children and that we have neither attempted to correct the wrong nor have we asked for forgiveness. What may be even worse than these three is not forgiving others that have wronged us. These emotions, along with anger, are all closely related. They all involve our relationship with other people and are triggered by an action or perception that one person has mistreated another. They are also similar because the worse the hurt, the more we can rationalize or justify our actions in the conflict. The longer we hold the resentment or guilt without acting to correct it, the more this separates us from God and His gift of peace.

First We Must Pray

So how do we restore our feeling of peace from God? The answer is the same as it is for any problem that keeps us separated from God. First, we must pray. We must talk to God and confess those sins that are most obvious to us. Second, we must repent of those sins. Third, we must "go and sin no more." You cannot lay hold of Christ while still clinging to your sin. Last, we must listen to God, and He will tell us what corrective actions we need to take. However, do not use this as an excuse to do nothing because you are still waiting for God to write down on stone tablets the precise actions you are to take. He may speak to you in many ways. He may already have spoken to you through your conscience. You may already know part of what you must do, but you will not see if you ignore your conscience. He also may speak to you through the Bible. You may discover "coincidentally" just the right scripture to direct your actions. However, if God is to reveal his answer through the Bible, you must read it regularly.

Other ways that God may speak to you are through a spouse, a friend, or even through the one you have wronged. Listen. Be aware of what God is trying to tell you, and then act. However, do not be surprised if, as soon as you have removed one problem that keeps you from accepting God's gift of peace, another pops up that you have long since forgotten. Do not despair. God is bringing you closer to Him each time you declare another layer of guilt or resentment and allow God to remove them. It is like the passage in the first chapter of James:

> *My brothers and sisters, whenever you face trials of any kind, consider it nothing but joy, because you know that the testing of your faith produces endurance; and let endurance have its full effect, so that you may be mature and complete, lacking in nothing* (James 1:2-4).

Remember, all things work for good for those that love the Lord, and as each layer of our trials is exposed, it is another opportunity to be God's witness in this world. It is another opportunity to become even closer to God and accept His gift of peace more completely.

Peace I leave with you; my peace I give you. I do not give to you as the world gives. Do not let your hearts be troubled and do not let them be afraid (John 14:27).

Which Scripture Has God Shown to You?

The first time I remember finding the first chapter of James particularly meaningful was when I had started a new business, and it was not going well. There were many trials and temptations to be "welcomed as friends," as the Phillips translation expresses the idea. If we are open to Him, God has a way to bring the particular scripture to us that will help us the most at each time of trial in our lives. Think of which scripture God had illuminated for you when you were in real need of His inner peace. Go back and read that scripture again. Can you feel His sense of inner peace flowing over you again? Does this sense of inner peace enhance your feeling of forgiveness? Read on.

Discussion:

1. Reread Matthew 5:44 – How can we be expected to love our enemies and pray for those who persecute us?

   _____

   _____

2. Reread Matthew 5:45 – Does this sound fair to you? __

3. In what situation is it most difficult for you to remain calm rather than react angrily and displace the feeling of God's peace within you? _____

   _____

   _____

   _____

4. Do you feel that you have accepted God's gift of "the peace that passes all understanding?"

   a. All the time _____

   b. Most of the time _____

   c. Only occasionally _____

   d. Never _____

   e. Explain your answers. _____

   _____

   _____

   _____

Call to Action:

1. Think of which scripture(s) God had illuminated for you when you were in real need of His inner peace. ____

   _____

2. Go back and read that scripture again. Can you feel God's sense of inner peace flowing over you again? Write about why you think this scripture has a positive effect on your sense of inner peace. _____

   _____

   _____

   _____

   _____

3. Does this sense of inner peace enhance your feeling of forgiveness? _____

   a. Explain. _____

   _____

   _____

   _____

Reading List, Forgiveness:

Matthew 6:1-18   Acts 26:1-32

Matthew18:15-20   Mark 11:20-25

Additional Scripture references:

_____

_____

Chapter 11, Forgiveness

Forgiveness is a concept that does not seem to be inherent in human nature. We have been taught to say, "Excuse me," when we do something that disturbs someone. For relatively insignificant things, the person disturbed might say something like, "Oh, that's OK," or "no real harm done." These expressions are primarily polite interchanges between two persons that may not even know each other. The forgiveness that I am talking about in this chapter is when we have really been hurt, more often emotionally rather than physically. In most cases, someone we know causes these hurts—maybe even a spouse or a close friend. The more we expect from someone or trust someone, the more likely it is that there will be a hurt that we feel is unforgivable when things go wrong. Experiences and feelings like this affect our relationship with the person that hurt us and frequently keep us from trusting other people in similar situations. When this happens, we withhold our total commitment to other relationships, diminishing our ability to live a whole life. We waste energy and make the hurt worse the longer it remains unforgiven.

God's Unconditional Forgiveness

It is only by allowing God to control our lives that we can unconditionally forgive others. Only when we have unconditionally forgiven others are we able to accept God's unconditional forgiveness for ourselves. Saying that we can or will forgive an act "if ..." is not what I am talking about. Whenever there is an "if" coupled with our forgiveness, it is not the unconditional forgiveness necessary for us to accept God's unconditional forgiveness for our sins. In the Lord's Prayer, we are told to ask for forgiveness—as we have already forgiven others (Matt. 6:12). In verses 14 and 15, Christ gets more specific.

> *For if you forgive men when they sin against*
> *you, your heavenly Father will also forgive you. But*
> *if you do not forgive men their sins, your Father*
> *will not forgive your sins* (Matt. 6:14-15, NIV).

Here it seems that Christ is telling us that God's forgiveness is conditional. There is an "if" associated with His forgiveness. Is that really what Christ is telling us? Is God's forgiveness conditional? Before I discuss what we need to do to find the intended meaning of this scripture, let me emphatically state, <u>God's forgiveness is not conditional!</u> However, we may be unable to accept His forgiveness.

Now, let's go back to the scripture. To find the intended meaning, we need to understand the context of this statement by Christ. Let us look at some more of the sixth chapter of Matthew. Christ is talking about our actual relationship with God, not the image that we present to others. This scripture tells us about hypocritical actions in praying, fasting, and all aspects of our claimed love of God, instead of our actual love of God. Christ is talking about situations when the outward show, which is only for other persons, is different from what God knows is in our heart. It is what we do in secret, which reveals our true selves. In this context, we can see Christ is telling us that to ask God for forgiveness without first forgiving anyone we have a grievance against would also be hypocritical, and there would be no reward in heaven. In other words, God's forgiveness is not conditional—it is our ability to accept His forgiveness, which is conditional. If we do not forgive others first, we are unable to accept God's forgiveness for ourselves. The following story illustrates the depth of forgiveness God is offering us and the need for our complete forgiveness of others.

Forgiveness

One day a while back, a man, his heart heavy with grief, was walking in the woods. As he thought about his life this day, he knew many things were not right. He thought about those who had lied about him back when he had a job.

His thoughts turned to those who had stolen his things and cheated him. He remembered his family that had passed on. His mind turned to the illness he had that no one could cure. Anger, resentment, and frustration filled his very soul.

Standing there this day, searching for answers he could not find, knowing all else had failed him, he knelt at the base of an old oak tree to seek the one he knew would always be there. With tears in his eyes, he prayed: "Lord - - - You have done wonderful things for me in this life. You have told me to do many things for you, and I happily obeyed. Today, you have told me to forgive. I am sad, Lord, because I cannot. I do not know-how. It is not fair Lord. I did not deserve the wrongs that were done against me, and I should not have to forgive. As perfect as your way is Lord, this one thing I cannot do, for I do not know how to forgive. My anger is so deep Lord, I fear I may not hear you, but I pray that you teach me to do this one thing I cannot do - - - Teach me To Forgive."

As he knelt there in the quiet shade of that old oak tree, he felt something fall onto his shoulder. He opened his eyes. Out of the corner of one eye, he saw something red on his shirt. He could not turn to see what it was because where the oak tree had been was a large square piece of wood in the ground. He raised his head and saw two feet held to the wood with a large spike through them. He raised his head more, and tears came to his eyes as he saw Jesus hanging on a cross. He saw spikes in His hands, a gash in His side, a torn and battered body, deep thorns sunk into His head. Finally, he saw the suffering and pain on His precious face. As their eyes met, the man's tears turned to sobbing, and Jesus began to speak.

Have you ever told a lie, he asked?

The man answered - - - yes Lord.

Have you ever been given too much change and kept it?

The man answered yes Lord. The man sobbed more and more.

Have you ever taken something from work that was not yours, Jesus asked?

The man answered yes Lord.

Have you ever sworn, using my Father's name in vain?

The man, crying now, answered yes Lord.

As Jesus asked many more times, "Have you ever?" The man's crying became uncontrollable, for he could only answer yes Lord.

Then Jesus turned His head from one side to the other, and the man felt something fall on his other shoulder. He looked and saw that it was the blood of Jesus. When he looked back up, his eyes met those of Jesus. They were full of love, like nothing the man had ever seen or known

Jesus said, I did not deserve this either, but I forgive you.

This story may seem a little gruesome and graphic. Sometimes we need to be shocked a little to get our attention. But, in truth, we are all responsible for a part of Christ's suffering. We all have sinned, and we all need to be washed in the redemptive blood of Christ. Also, we all need to forgive others who have hurt us so that we can accept the redemption that Christ is offering us.

Old Testament Forgiveness

Forgiveness is not just a New Testament concept. In Leviticus, we read what the Law of Moses said a person must do to receive forgiveness for their sins against each other. For every individual sin a person at any station might commit, there was a list of what the person needed to sacrifice. There were also instructions on how to perform that sacrifice. Following these to the letter would allow the person to earn God's forgiveness. The Mosaic Law recognized that there was a cost to others when we sinned and made the assumption that if we physically sacrifice something equally important, we would realize what we had done to someone else and God and repent of that sin. To make sure that the sacrifice specified was at an appropriate cost to the sinner, each item listed in the sacrifice was to be "without blemish." It was to be the best of the flock, the best of the herd, or the best of the crop. The sacrificed item was not the place to get rid of your discards or culls.

Many of the writers in the New Testament remind us that the Mosaic Law did not work. God may have forgiven people, but they did not change their lives, and no redemption occurred. You cannot earn the forgiveness that Christ talks about; it is a gift from God. However, for His forgiveness to be effective in our lives, we must be repentant of the sins we are asking to be forgiven. Moreover, we must not withhold our forgiveness from someone who has sinned against us. That is a sin in and of its self.

Repentance – Forgiveness – Acceptance

In Chapter 26 of Acts, Paul is defending himself in front of King Agrippa. As a part of this defense, he relates one of the most dramatic acts of repentance, forgiveness, acceptance, and receiving an assignment from God that we can find in the Bible.

> *I was traveling to Damascus with the authority and commission of the chief priests, when at midday along the road, your Excellency, I saw a light from heaven, brighter than the sun, shining around me and my companions. When we had all fallen to the ground, I heard a voice saying to me in the Hebrew language, 'Saul, Saul, why are you persecuting me? It hurts you to kick against the goads.' (It is hard for you when you work against God) I asked, 'Who are you, Lord?' The Lord answered, 'I am Jesus whom you are persecuting. But get up and stand on your feet; for I have appeared to you for this purpose, to appoint you to serve and testify to the things in which you have seen me and to those in which I will appear to you. I will rescue you from your people and from the Gentiles--to whom I am sending you to open their eyes so that they may turn from darkness to light and from the power of Satan to God, so that they may receive forgiveness of sins and a place among those who are sanctified by faith in me.*
> (Acts 26:12b-18).

After relating this absolutely fantastic experience with Christ, Paul tells the King: "Yes, I did what I am charged with." He confessed to the charges because he had done, and was doing, what God had commanded him to do. In Paul's words:

> *After that, King Agrippa, I was not disobedient to the heavenly vision, but declared first to those in Damascus, then in Jerusalem and throughout the countryside of Judea, and also to the Gentiles, that they should repent and turn to God and do deeds consistent with repentance.*
> (Acts 26:19-20).

In this dramatic conversion, Saul, the Jewish henchman on a mission with authority to seek and destroy Christians even in their own homes, becomes Paul, the Christian evangelist to the world. Without the gift of forgiveness, Paul could never have performed God's mission. He would have been overcome with the guilt of his past life and powerless to do God's will. Instead, in a relatively short period, Paul saw his vision of God in the form of Christ, was blinded, realized what he was doing was wrong, and repented. He accepted God's forgiveness, regained his sight, and began to accept God's will for him in his life.

No Reservations

Our repentance for our past sins and our acceptance of God's forgiveness has probably not been as dramatic as Paul's was. However, we can learn from Paul's experience and apply it to our own lives is—that only by completely accepting God's forgiveness can we be effective in finding and doing God's will in our own lives. It seems that it should be easy to accept forgiveness, but to accept God's forgiveness for ourselves—we must have no reservations in our forgiveness for anyone else. Let me repeat that:

We must have absolutely no reservations in our forgiveness for anyone else!

The process of removing all of our current and past reservations and forgiving those seemingly unforgivable acts that someone has done to us may be like peeling an onion; as we remove one layer, God reveals another. However, unlike an onion that gets smaller and has less substance each time you remove a layer, we become more significant, with more to offer to the world around us, as we let go of past hurts and allow God to work through us. There will be a point when we have finally forgiven all the unforgivable things that have happened to us over our lifetime. Moreover, each time we allow God's love to work through us and forgive another, we are a little less likely to hold on to those events of today that could become our resentments of tomorrow. That is not something that you can do using just your own will. Maybe some of them you can, but the strength and understanding needed to take away those hurts we have harbored and rationalized about for so long can only come from God. We need to pray to God, asking Him for the strength and the understanding we need to forgive the old hurts. We must stop rationalizing why we cannot, or should not, forgive and listen to what God is telling us about our own need to forgive. Yes, we are the ones that will benefit the most when we finally do forgive those acts that we have considered unforgivable for so long. God will lift the burden from our hearts that will allow us to accept His forgiveness for our sins.

Are You Binding Someone Else to Sin?

There is another aspect of our forgiving that Catherine Marshall illuminates in her book "Something More." It comes from her understanding of the following scripture verse.

Truly I tell you, whatever you bind on earth will be bound in heaven, and whatever you loose on earth will be loosed in heaven (Mat 18:18).

Her understanding of this scripture was that if a believer does not forgive someone who has sinned against them but hangs onto their judgment of that person, this can bind the offender to the conditions you would like to see changed. Although some interpretations of this particular scripture believe the word "you" refers to the church rather than an individual, the idea that our not forgiving can bind another to their sins certainly places another incentive to be forgiving.

In the same book, Catherine Marshall tells about times when her prayer life was not what she thought it should be. She described it as "one of those prayers-not-getting-beyond-the-ceiling periods." Thinking about scriptures like Mark 11:22-24, she prays for God to increase her faith. She feels that her faith must be inadequate, or else her prayers would be more fruitful. When God answered her prayers for more faith, He told her that a lack of faith was not the problem. The problem was that she was holding on to hurts from others that she needed to forgive. Cathrine needed to read one more verse in Mark. In addition to Chapter 11, verses 22-24, she also needed to read verse 25.

> *Jesus answered them: "Have faith in God. Truly I tell you, if you say to this mountain, 'Be taken up and thrown into the sea,' and if you do not doubt in your heart, but believe that what you say will come to pass, it will be done for you. So I tell you, whatever you ask for in prayer, believe that you have received it, and it will be yours. <u>Whenever you stand praying, forgive, if you have anything against anyone; so that your Father in heaven may also forgive you your trespasses."</u>*
> (Mark 11:22-25).

Because of God's answer to her prayers, she and her husband started a systematic process. Every morning, they would spend thirty minutes in separate rooms listing all the hurts they were harboring, writing each on an individual piece of paper, going back as far as they could remember. After creating their lists, they would come together and pray aloud to forgive each offender, thereby releasing themselves from that hurt. Once they prayed for each person and hurt, they tore up that piece of paper and put the pieces in a manila envelope. Eventually, they burned the envelope and its contents. These lists were exhaustive; they even included persons that Catherine Marshall had never met. Like people she had only read about but still had made judgments about what they had done, even when it did not directly affect her.

God Will Help Us Remember

When we start to clean out our closets, God will keep reminding us of what is left and the actions we need to take, if we will listen to Him. He wants our lives' closets to be clean so that we can live the fullest life possible.

What is it in your life that you have been unable to forgive? First, pray about the problems and the person or persons involved. Then, ask God to help you accept His love within you to show that love and allow you to forgive the hurt you have been harboring. That will not be easy but, when done, you will be able to accept God's forgiveness for yourself and lift burdens that you may have been carrying around for a long time. Believe God loves you and believe that, with His love, you can forgive even the most unforgivable act.

Discussion:

1. Discuss the relationships between the following words: Conversion, repentance, and forgiveness. _____

   _____

   _____

2. What is different between the Old Testament approach to forgiveness and the New Testament approach? _____

   _____

3. Make a list of anyone in your life that you need to forgive and have not. _____

   _____

4. Take the above list and write out what you need to forgive and why you have not. _____

   _____

   _____

   _____

   _____

   _____

   _____

Call to Action:

1. Add the persons and situations from numbers three and four above to your regular prayer list. Ask God to help you forgive each person on your list. Then, record your list and God's responses in your journal.

2. As you have forgiven some on your list, add to your journal any additional problems that God reveals to you that require your forgiveness.

3. Are there those that you still do not seem to be able to forgive? You may need to set aside a particular time of prayer just for this if you are having trouble forgiving everyone. Ask God to help you accept His love within you to show that love and truly forgive the hurt you have been harboring.

Reading List, Prophecy:

Acts 2:1-24   1 Corinthians 12:1-31
1 Corinthians 14:1-39   James 2:14-26

Additional Scripture references:

_____

_____

Chapter 12, Prophecy

In the Old Testament, prophecy generally identifies a predictive type of speech. The prophets told what was going to happen to Israel based on their current actions. That was most often a prediction of bad things that God would cause to happen because Israel had followed their typical pattern, taken up the pagan practices of those around them, and ceased to follow God. In the New Testament, we start with the same idea that prophecy is a statement of what will happen. It represents a gift of the ability to see into the future but generally, on a cause and effect basis, which indicates that the actual skill of the prophets, both Old and New Testament, was one of knowing, and communicating with, God. They were able to hear God, understand God, and relate His message to the people of Israel. The dictionary definition of prophecy includes: 1) speaking as if divinely inspired; 2) giving instruction in religious matters, i.e. preaching; and 3) making a prediction. Those first two definitions, which are much broader than just predicting, are how I see Paul using the word prophecy in the New Testament.

Not Just Foretelling the Future

In the second chapter of Acts, the writer tells us the story of Pentecost, the day when the Holy Spirit empowered the apostles. This power enabled them to speak so that each person present heard the message in their primary language. After Pentecost and the coming of the Holy Spirit, the word prophecy is used to describe a somewhat different kind of speech. Starting with verse 17:

> *In the last days, God says, I will pour out my*
> *Spirit on all people. Your sons and daughters will*
> *prophesy, your young men will see visions, your old*
> *men will dream dreams. Even on my servants, both*
> *men and women, I will pour out my Spirit in those*
> *days, and they will prophesy* (Acts 2:17-18, NIV).

We are no longer just talking about foretelling the future—the apostles tell the story of Christ, His crucifixion, and His resurrection. However, we are talking about speech that represents knowledge and understanding of God. Starting again at verse 22, we hear part of what they are saying:

> *Men of Israel, listen to this: Jesus of Nazareth*
> *was a man accredited by God to you by miracles,*
> *wonders and signs, which God did among you*
> *through him, as you yourselves know. This man was*
> *handed over to you by God's set purpose and*
> *foreknowledge; and you, with the help of wicked*
> *men, put him to death by nailing him to the cross.*
> *But God raised him from the dead, freeing him from*
> *the agony of death, because it was impossible for*
> *death to keep its hold on him* (Acts 2:22-24, NIV).

Prophecy is the Gift to be Most Desired

That represents what has been the real mark of prophecy throughout the entire Bible. Prophecy is the uttering of words to the community that reveal an understanding of what God is trying to do through you. It is informative and instructive as to God's plan but not necessarily a foretelling of the future. That is why Paul said in 1 Corinthians 14: "The gift of prophecy is the gift of the Spirit that is to be most desired." Paul says he emphasizes prophecy because it helps the community members understand God's plan for their community and helps each individual understand their part in God's plan.

So, where are we likely to find prophecy today? A sermon may prophecy; a discussion about how God interacts with us may include prophecy; a person standing on the street corner declaring their understanding of how God wants the world to change may be prophecy. There is no simple way that we can determine whether what we are hearing is prophecy or not. We cannot just accept the word of the person claiming to be a prophet. Neither can we use a person's position in the community or standing in the church to determine whether they are speaking prophetically. You cannot obtain a degree or position that ensures what a person is saying is prophetic. In addition, we cannot assume because of where we hear the purported prophecy that it is or is not. It is each individual's responsibility to determine whether what they hear is or is not prophecy. How do we do that? We must test it against the Bible, try it against reason, hold it up to tradition, and ultimately, listen to what the Holy Spirit reveals to us. We must evaluate everything that we receive to determine whether it is a genuine message from God. There is a story about Socrates that gives us a starting point for evaluation of what we hear. This story demonstrates his wisdom on a secular basis, but if we use the Bible and the Holy Spirit to evaluate the "truth test," it all becomes very biblical.

Socrates and the Triple Filter Test

In ancient Greece, Socrates was reputed to hold knowledge in high esteem. One day, an acquaintance met the great philosopher and said,

"Do you know what I just heard about your friend?"

"Hold on a minute," Socrates replied. "Before telling me anything, I'd like you to pass a little test. It's called the Triple Filter Test."

"Triple filter?"

"That's right," Socrates continued. "Before you talk to me about my friend, it might be a good idea to take a moment and filter what you're going to say. That is why I call it the triple filter test.

The first filter is Truth. Have you made absolutely sure that what you are about to tell me is true?"

"No," the man said, "actually, I just heard about it and."

"All right," said Socrates. "So you don't really know if it's true or not. Now let us try the second filter, the filter of Goodness. Is what you are about to tell me about my friend something good?"

"No, on the contrary..."

"So," Socrates continued, "you want to tell me something bad about him, but you're not certain it's true. You may still pass the test though, because there is one filter left: the filter of Usefulness.

Is what you want to tell me about my friend going to be useful to me?

"No, not really...."

"Well," concluded Socrates, "if what you want to tell me is neither true nor good nor even useful, why tell it to me at all?"

That is good advice for each of us in filtering what we might be tempted to say. It also applies to what we hear, as much of what we hear would not pass the "Triple Filter Test." Like Socrates, we should ask, why should I listen? Of course, our standard for prophetic speech is much higher. Ideas that we hear must pass the "Bible Test" before we can consider them prophetic. That is, they must be consistent with the truths in the Bible. Of course, if we are going to use the Bible's truths to test whether someone's ideas are prophetic, that means that we must have some knowledge of the Bible.

Use It in Proportion to Your Faith

In Chapter 4, I talked about the different gifts of the Spirit. One of those gifts that were identified was the gift of prophecy. In Romans, Paul tells us:

If a man's gift is prophesying, let him use it in proportion to his faith (Rom. 12:7, NIV).

Then, in 1 Corinthians:

Now to each one the manifestation of the Spirit is given for the common good. To one there is given through the Spirit the message of wisdom, to another the message of knowledge by means of the same Spirit, to another faith by the same Spirit, to another gifts of healing by that one Spirit, to another miraculous powers, to another prophecy, to another distinguishing between Spirits, to another speaking in different kinds of tongues, and to still another the interpretation of tongues (1 Cor. 12:7-10, NIV).

In Romans, Paul is talking about prophecy in the context of being humble; use it in proportion to your faith. Then, in 1 Corinthians, he reminds the believers in Corinth that all gifts of the Spirit must be used for the "common good." Both of these texts help us to identify the gift of prophecy. If persons purporting to be prophesying are going beyond their faith, as evidenced by other aspects of their lives, their words are suspect. In addition, if a message claimed to be prophetic does not serve to enlighten the general church community, it is suspect. Just believing in God or being knowledgeable about

God and the scripture is insufficient to identify the speaker as credible. As James told us:

> *You believe that there is one God. Good! Even*
> *the demons believe that--and shudder*
> (James 2:19, NIV).

If we look at the list of spiritual gifts from the twelfth chapter of 1 Corinthians, we notice that gift of the message of wisdom, the gift of the message of knowledge, and the gift of prophecy are specifically listed. The New Jerusalem translation of the Bible explains that the gift of uttering the message of wisdom is probably a gift of preaching the most profound Christian truths about God and God's life within us. The explanation given for the gift of uttering the message of knowledge is that it is probably the preaching of elementary Christian truths. From this, we might conclude that the reference to prophecy is a gift of prediction, as preaching seems covered by the gifts of wisdom and knowledge. However, if we look at the complete list, we see that the list includes the gifts of healing and miraculous powers. Surely all of the gifts, healing, speaking in tongues, interpreting, etc., are all miraculous powers, which indicate that each gift listed does not singularly identify a unique gift. It seems there is overlap between many of them, which would also be valid for the gift of prophecy relative to the gifts of uttering the message of wisdom and the message of knowledge.

A Manifestation of the Holy Spirit

These gifts are manifestations of the Holy Spirit working within you, and many might occur as a part of the same event. A good sermon would likely use all three of the gifts of wisdom, knowledge, and prophecy. It might start with fundamental Christian truths based on the "knowledge" of the preacher, continue with deeper Christian truths based on the "wisdom" of the preacher, and then, include a prophetic message from the personal experiences of the preacher's relationship to, and understanding of, how God is working in the community. The sermon may even include the foretelling of God's plan for the future. That may be too much for today's twenty-minute sermon, but if you read the sermons of great preachers of the past like John Wesley, all of these elements are likely to be present.

For a person to be capable of prophecy, there must first be an indwelling of the Holy Spirit and the speaker's reliance on this inspiration. There is a story about a preacher who knew about the Holy Spirit's power but was not accustomed to relying on this power on a regular basis. Most likely, his sermons did not include any prophetic messages.

Not a Prophet

A preacher worked hard on his sermon most of the week and retyped it on Saturday night. During the night, his dog chewed it all up. He did not notice this until it was time to go to church. When he got in the pulpit, he said, "I had a nice sermon prepared for you this morning, but my dog chewed it up. I'm going to have to rely on the inspiration of the Holy Spirit today, but I promise to do better next Sunday."

We do not know whether the preacher in this story related his lack of understanding of the Holy Spirit and how it worked in his life or whether he just spoke before he thought. It does not make any difference, as the story's point is to show how sometimes, we all tend to rely on our skills rather than let the Holy Spirit work through these skills. As I indicated before the story, we can be sure that there will be no prophetic speech from our mouths unless and until the Holy Spirit is at work in both the preparation and the presentation of any message. Paul said that we should strive for the gift of prophecy. He is not telling us that there is a way to work harder, and then we will become a prophet. Paul is saying to us today that we need to be open to the gifts of the Holy Spirit.

Use the Gift for God's Glory

If the gift of prophecy is one we receive, we should accept it and use it to God's glory. Of course, like all of God's gifts, there is the implied message that we do not just stand up one day and start speaking prophetically. We must start at the beginning. We must recognize, believe, and accept that God loved us so much that Christ died for our salvation. We must also believe that when Christ returned to be with God, the Holy Spirit came to indwell each believer with powers that will glorify God and help bring His kingdom to all when they are accepted and appropriately used. What better relationship could we ever desire with God than to be spreading His "Good News" by allowing the Holy Spirit within us to utter messages of knowledge and wisdom while speaking prophetically about our understanding of what God wants our community of faith to accomplish?

Discussion:

1. Referring to 1 Corinthians 14, why do you think Paul prefers prophesying to the other gifts of the Spirit? _____

    _____

    _____

2. Do you think that Paul is only talking about foretelling the future when he talks about prophecies? Explain. _____

    _____

    _____

3. What is your definition of prophecy? _____

    _____

    _____

4. Within that definition, do you or have you ever known anyone with the gift of prophecy? How did you know?

    _____

    _____

    _____

Call to Action:

1. Is prophecy one of your gifts? Pray about how God wants you to witness "The Good News" in your life. Record your prayer and the answers in your journal

Reading List, Witness:

John 1:1-23   Acts 1:12-26

Acts 14:1-28   Acts 22:1-26

Additional Scripture references:

_____

_____

Chapter 13, Witness

In some ways, witnessing is not a gift by itself. It is the result of how we use all the other gifts we have received from God. One difference may be in how we define witness. We are always witnessing, regardless of how much or little we follow God's will in our lives. God's gift for witnessing is what we need to effectively spread the Good News and let those around us know the importance and the effect of our relationship with God.

A Man Sent from God

Our witness may be positive or negative; it could also be a "false witness." Chapter 1 of the Gospel of John shows the first example of the type of witness about which I am talking. This witness was a gift from God.

> *There was a man sent from God, whose name was John. He came as a witness to testify to the light, so that all might believe through him. He himself was not the light, but he came to testify to the light* (John 1:6-8).

John the Baptist was an ordinary man. He did extraordinary things. As I said in Chapter 3, the angel told his father, Zechariah, John would be filled with the Holy Spirit from birth. We can also be filled with the Holy Spirit and do extraordinary things. As near as we can tell, all of John's adult life was dedicated to doing God's will by following what the angel revealed to Zechariah about John's life mission. For John, that meant denying himself of any earthly pleasures and preparing the way for Christ. As the Gospel says, he was sent from God! We are all "sent from God." The difference is that John listened and did what God wanted him to do. John was God's witness to God's unfolding plan: he was the witness to the coming Messiah.

Repentance, Forgiveness

You might think that the Messiah would be a popular thing to be talking about in John's time. The Jews looked forward to the coming of the Messiah and frequently talked about how, when the Messiah came, all their troubles would go away. There is a scene in the play "Fiddler on the Roof" that demonstrated this. It begins when a trusted government representative tells them they have only three days to sell their homes and leave Anastasia. For most of the residents, this is the only place they have ever lived, and even though it certainly is not a paradise, they do not want to leave. The men of the town are all gathered, discussing the situation, and one of the men asks the Rabbi, "Wouldn't this be a good time for the Messiah to come?" They expected the Messiah to be a physical ruler, take charge, and protect the Jews from the government's persecution. However, John was not witnessing to the kind of Messiah that the Hebrews wanted or expected. John talked about repentance and forgiveness. Even worse, He was not just talking about God forgiving the Jews. He told the Jews that they need to forgive others as well. John talked about their personal sins. He told the Jews what each one of them needed to do personally in preparation for the Messiah. John was not talking about a Messiah that would put down the Romans and put the Jews in charge. He spoke about a Messiah that would change their lives and change how they related to God and each other.

The Jews had a lot of wishful thinking in their idea of what the Messiah should and would be. They were tired of everyone kicking them around, and they were looking for the Messiah to come and see that they received their proper rewards for being faithful to God. The problem was, as a group, they really had not been very faithful. Therefore, in actuality, they were receiving their proper rewards, oppression by the Romans. That is what John was telling them, and it was not what they wanted to hear. As a result, John's witness was not popular. In fact, in the end, it cost him his life.

Although John spoke his words around 2,000 years ago, they are as appropriate for believers today as when John said them. We still need to hear them today. John's message was not just to prepare the way for Christ in His first physical appearance. All people need his message of repentance today and every day of our lives. As Paul tells us, all have sinned and fallen short of the glory of God, not just once but throughout our lives. Each day we need to listen to what John had to say. "Prepare the way for Christ in our lives. Repent!"

How you Make Decisions is Part of Your Witness

Another kind of witnessing I want to talk about is the witnessing that occurred after Christ's ministry, crucifixion, and resurrection. Just before the day of Pentecost, the remaining eleven disciples decided that they needed to replace Judas to maintain the same number of apostles as Christ had selected.

> So they proposed two, Joseph called Barsabbas, who was also known as Justus, and Matthias. Then they prayed and said, "Lord, you know everyone's heart. Show us which one of these two you have chosen to take the place in this ministry and apostleship from which Judas turned aside to go to his own place." And they cast lots for

169

them, and the lot fell on Matthias; and he was added to the eleven apostles (Acts 1:23-26).

Christ had selected twelve disciples, and the remaining eleven felt that they needed to maintain that same number of witnesses to Christ's resurrection. They chose from those that had been with Christ for most of His ministry and sorted them down to two possibilities. Then, the scripture says they prayed to let God make the final selection. I suspect that there had also been many prayers as the remaining eleven disciples made the initial selections. However, they left the final selection of the twelfth witness totally in God's hands. Those eleven disciples knew that God would choose between the last two candidates by controlling the casting of lots to ensure the selection of the proper person. The direct involvement of God in the selection of the twelfth witness indicated the importance the disciples gave to witnessing. In this example, they were witnessing by how they made the decisions in their lives. God was completely involved in this decision and we can be sure that God was also involved in most decisions the apostles made.

Telling the Good News

The next time we see a lot about witnessing is in the book of Acts. From this point on, the New Testament is primarily about witnessing. It is about the apostles and other followers telling the Good News. However, witnessing in this time was not without risk! Paul and Barnabas had witnessed to both Jew and Gentile. Because of the success of their witness, they were driven out of Antioch, Iconium, Lycaonia, etc. Chapter 14 of Acts shows us how Paul responded to intimidation while he was witnessing.

The same thing occurred in Iconium, where Paul and Barnabas went into the Jewish synagogue and spoke in such a way that a great number of both Jews and Greeks became believers. But the *unbelieving Jews stirred up the Gentiles and poisoned their minds against the brothers. <u>So they remained for a long time, speaking boldly for the Lord,</u> who testified to the word of his grace by granting signs and wonders to be done through them* (Acts 14:1-3).

Not everyone believed, even though the Lord was working wonders through Paul and Barnabas. Those who did not believe were not happy. To continue:

And when an attempt was made by both Gentiles and Jews, with their rulers, to mistreat them and to stone them, the apostles learned of it and fled to Lystra and Derbe, cities of Lycaonia, and to the surrounding country; and there they continued proclaiming the good news (Acts 14:5-7).

Many, in particular the Jewish leaders, had a lot to lose if everyone believed that Christ was indeed the Messiah. They were the power brokers of the time, and that position would be lost. As we see today, by inciting a crowd, others will do the dirty work for you. Nevertheless, this did not deter the great witnesses of the day. Paul continued to witness regardless of what the authorities did to him. As we see in the following four verses Acts 14, the Lord was with him in his witness.

In Lystra, there was a man sitting who could not use his feet and had never walked, for he had been crippled from birth. He listened to Paul as he was speaking. And Paul, looking at him intently and seeing that he had faith to be healed, said in a loud voice, "Stand upright on your feet." And the man sprang up and began to walk. When the crowds saw what Paul had done, they shouted in the Lycaonian language, "The gods have come down to us in human form!" (Acts 14:8-11).

Satan Was Enticing Paul

The story in these four verses shows us several things about Paul. First, he was very aware and perceptive about the persons around him. He could tell that the disabled man had the faith necessary for Paul to enable his healing. Second, Paul knew that the Lord had given him the power of healing, and he knew how and when it was appropriate to use it. Third, there were tremendous temptations for Paul. Satan, through the people, was enticing him to believe that rather than being God's agent doing God's will, he was himself a god. Lastly, you can tell that the miracle of healing was a great attention getter for the people, but it did not get the entire message across. Paul had more work to do, more witnessing to the source of his power, which was God working through him. Not that Paul was a god, which the people wanted to declare, but The God was working through Paul. Paul was witnessing to the One and Only God of all people and all things. Paul was witnessing to the Creator as the power through which he was able to perform miraculous acts.

Next, we find Paul defending himself in a Roman court because he has threatened the powers of the Jewish leadership by his witnessing about Christ. First, he tells them his background, what he had been, just like them, a zealot to destroy the Christians. Then, he tells them that he had been wrong and that God had revealed the truth to him personally. Not surprisingly, this did not go over very well. However, that did not deter Paul. Christ had shown Paul the light, and he was going to follow it wherever it took him. Paul would do whatever Christ directed him to do. And what Christ told Paul was – he was to be the witness to the entire world!

> *Then he said, "The God of our ancestors has chosen you to know his will, to see the Righteous One and to hear his own voice; for you will be his witness to all the world of what you have seen and heard. And now why do you delay? Get up, be*

172

baptized, and have your sins washed away, calling on his name" (Acts 22:14-16).

No Time for Excuses

God told Paul: *"Now why do you delay?"* In other words, forget your excuses; forget what you are not able to do. Instead, trust in the Lord to empower you for whatever situation that He gives you!

The greatest good that God can work through each one of us is to "go and make disciples of all men." Christ commanded us to witness to all the people around us about how He is working in our lives. Because Christ commanded us to witness, we will never be completely following God's will for our lives until we are witnessing to all persons with whom we come in contact.

Paul refused to make excuses for what he knew was God's work. God is telling us the same thing. We are not to make excuses about why we cannot witness or worry about how to witness. We just need to let everyone we meet see how God is working in our lives. God desires to build a testimony within us that will reflect His power acting in and through us. An essential part of our witness is letting those we work with or socialize with see His strength working within us. The experiences in our lives create our witness. How we allow God to work in our lives, through these experiences, determines how much of the nature and character of Christ others will see in us. Sometimes these experiences are devastating but, when we allow God to bring good out of these disastrous events, He can reveal His power in even greater ways. As Paul said, God's witness is made greater through our weaknesses.

We are Always Witnessing

What we must remember is—we cannot choose whether to witness or not to witness. We are continually witnessing. The nature of our witness changes dependent upon our relationship with God. We are continually witnessing as to how we have exercised the free will that God gave us. When our witness is one of anger and conflict, it can have lasting negative results on those around us. A prime example is what physical and verbal abuse in a marriage can do to the children of that marriage. In the words of an African proverb: "When the elephants fight, it's the grass that suffers."

How we look at ordinary events, like a school lesson, can trigger a significant witness to others. But, do we start the day thinking about what our witness will be that day? Or do we only think about our witness when we see someone else giving either a particularly positive or a particularly negative witness? The following story about a group of students illustrates how our vision of life can affect those around us.

The (Real) Seven Wonders of the World

A teacher asks a group of students to list what they thought were the present "Seven Wonders of the World."

Though there were some disagreements, the following received the most votes: Egypt's Great Pyramids, Taj Mahal, Grand Canyon, Panama Canal, Empire State Building, St. Peter's Basilica, and China's Great Wall.

While gathering the votes, the teacher noted that one student had not finished her paper yet. So she asked the girl if she was having trouble with her list. The girl replied, "Yes, a little. I couldn't quite make up my mind because there were so many."

The teacher said, "Well, tell us what you have, and maybe we can help."

The girl hesitated, then read, "I think the 'Seven Wonders of the World' are: To See, To Hear, To Touch, To Taste, To Feel, To Laugh, and To Love."

The room was so quiet you could have heard a pin drop. The things we overlook as simple and ordinary and that we take for granted are truly wondrous! A gentle reminder -- that the most precious things in life cannot be built by hand or bought by man; they have been given to us by God.

This one girl had a different view of life than the teacher or any of the other students. She saw God-given life as the most wondrous part of her world. It was so awesome that she was having trouble limiting it to just seven aspects of her life. Her witness that day was that life itself was the most important and wondrous part of the world.

If you doubt the potential effect of your witness, listen to what John Wesley said about witnessing.

"Give me one hundred men who fear nothing but God, who hate nothing but sin, and who know nothing but Jesus Christ and Him crucified, and I will shake (revolutionize) the world."

Are You Part of the Solution or Part of the Problem?

Does our witness tell others that we are a part of Christ's revolution, or does it tell them that we are the ones whose lives require revolution? Are we a missionary or a mission field? We need to pray that Christ will take away all hesitance and resistance to totally committing our lives to Him. We need to ask that He empower our lives so we may be a vehicle for Him to bring His good to those around us through our witness.

God has called each of us to a purpose greater than we understand. Know that it will require death to give life to this purpose. It must be His life that lives within us, not our own.

Discussion:

1. Talk about some examples of witnessing today that might be life-threatening. _____

   _____

   _____

2. How important is it to you that you consciously witness to people around you? _____

   _____

   _____

3. How important do you think your witness is to the people around you?

   a. Your family. _____

      _____

   b. Your friends. _____

      _____

   c. Strangers. _____

      _____

4. List any negative images in your witness that you would like to change. _____

   _____

5. List the most positive images that can be observed from your witness _____

   _____

6. Write your testimony. (Attach a copy to this workbook and your journal.

Call to Action:

1. Pray that Christ will take away all hesitance and resistance to totally committing your life to Him.

2. Ask that He empower your life that you may be a vehicle for Him to bring His good to those around you through your witness.

Reading List, Eternal Life:

John 3:1-21	Matthew 19:16-30
Matthew 25:31-46	Luke 10:25-37
Romans 6:20-23	1 Corinthians 2:6-16

Additional Scripture references:

_____

_____

Chapter 14, Eternal Life

The culmination of all of God's promises is the promise of eternal life. I started this series talking about the gift of Christ and salvation as the evidence of God's Love. The same verse, John 3:16, makes both promises. Even though this verse is probably the most quoted and memorized verse in the New Testament (it is available for people to read in over 1100 languages), we sometimes forget the setting for this statement about God's Love and eternal life. Let us look again at that setting. Nicodemus has told Jesus that he knows Jesus must be from God because of His demonstrated abilities. Then Jesus talks about being "Born Again." As we see in the scripture below, Nicodemus does not have a clue what Christ is talking about and asks another question indicating his misunderstanding. Christ then answers with more explanation.

> *Jesus answered him, "Very truly, I tell you, no one can see the kingdom of God without being born from above." Nicodemus said to him, "How can anyone be born after having grown old? Can one enter a second time into the mother's womb and be born?" Jesus answered, "Very truly, I tell you, no one can enter the kingdom of God without being born of water and Spirit. What is born of the flesh is flesh, and what is born of the Spirit is Spirit. Do not be astonished that I said to you; You must be born from above. The wind blows where it chooses, and*

you hear the sound of it, but you do not know where it comes from or where it goes. So it is with everyone who is born of the Spirit" (John 3:3-8).

Have Faith and Believe

Christ's answer is still a little mysterious for Nicodemus. He still cannot identify with the analogies that Christ has used. Because of Nicodemus's lack of understanding, Christ first chastises him for being a "teacher of Israel" and not understanding spiritual things. Then Christ tells him that if he does not understand, he just has to have a little faith and believe.

> *If I have told you about earthly things and you do not believe, how can you believe if I tell you about heavenly things? No one has ascended into heaven except the one who descended from heaven, the Son of Man. And just as Moses lifted up the serpent in the wilderness, so must the Son of Man be lifted up, that whoever believes in him may have eternal life* (John 3:12-15).

In this passage, Christ not only emphasizes the need for faith, but He also speaks about his authority, *"no one has ascended into heaven except...,"* and the necessity of His resurrection. Eternal life cannot be discussed outside of the context of the gift of Resurrection. God's gift of His Son that can lead to our eternal life included several parts. First, the impregnation of Mary by the Holy Spirit. Then His birth, His baptism by John, His ministry, and His betrayal by Judas. Followed by His Crucifixion, the acceptance of all our sins, His death, and descending into hell. And lastly, His Resurrection. The apparent lack of understanding of many of these aspects of God's gift left Nicodemus confused. He was certainly not the only one that did not understand what was necessary for eternal life then or now.

In Matthew and the other three Gospels, we have the story of the rich young ruler. In this case, the young ruler already knows and accepts that eternal life is possible; and he at least believes that he has lived his life according to the Mosaic Law. He also probably assumes that when he tells Jesus that he has always followed the law that Jesus will say that is enough. However, Christ knows what is in his heart and what is keeping the young man from being totally committed to doing God's will. It is his earthly possessions! Therefore, Christ tells him how to be perfect. We can tell that what Christ perceived in the man was accurate because the rich young ruler cannot part with what separates him from God.

> *Jesus said to him, "If you wish to be perfect, go, sell your possessions, and give the money to the poor, and you will have treasure in heaven; then come, follow me." When the young man heard this word, he went away grieving, for he had many possessions* (Matt. 19:21-22).

Whatever Separates You from God, Give It Up

The message is not that a person with earthly possessions can not get to heaven or even necessarily about possessions at all. The message is that you must give up whatever is more important to you than God. God must be first in our lives before we can accept all of His promises. He must be first in our lives before John 3:16 can move, from a promise that God makes to us to the gift of eternal life that we have accepted. As was indicated in Chapter 1, we have to get our priorities straight. Repeating the words of Christ as recorded in Matthew:

> *But seek first his kingdom and his righteousness, and all these things will be given to you as well.* (Matt. 6:33, NIV).

A little later in the twenty-fifth chapter of Matthew, Christ tells us the consequences of not obeying His commands.

And these will go away into eternal punishment, but the righteous into eternal life (Matt. 25:46).

The following story demonstrates in earthly values what we can lose by not desiring and paying the price to have Christ in our lives.

Take My Son

A wealthy man and his son loved to collect rare works of art. They had everything in their collection, from Picasso to Raphael. They would often sit together and admire the great works of art. When the Vietnam conflict broke out, the son went to war. He was very courageous and died in battle while rescuing another soldier. The father was notified and grieved deeply for his only son. About a month later, just before Christmas, there was a knock at the door. A young man stood at the door with a large package in his hands. He said, "Sir, you don't know me, but I am the soldier for whom your son gave his life. He saved many lives that day, and he was carrying me to safety when a bullet struck him in the heart, and he died instantly. He often talked about you and your love for art." The young man held out this package. "I know this isn't much. I'm not really a great artist, but I think your son would have wanted you to have this."

The father opened the package. It was a portrait of his son, painted by the young man. He stared in awe at how the soldier had captured the personality of his son in the painting. The father was so drawn to the eyes that his own eyes welled up with tears. He thanked the young man and offered to pay him for the picture. "Oh, no sir, I could never repay what your son did for me. It's a gift." The father hung the portrait over his mantle. Every time visitors came to his home, he took them to see the portrait of his son before he showed them any of the other great works he had collected.

The man died a few months later. There was to be a great auction of his paintings. Many influential people gathered, excited over seeing the great paintings and having an opportunity to purchase one for their collection. On the platform sat the painting of the son. The auctioneer pounded his gavel. "We will start the bidding with this picture of the son. Who will bid for this picture?" There was silence. Then a voice in the back of the room shouted, "We want to see the famous paintings. Skip this one." Never less, the auctioneer persisted. "Will someone bid for this painting? Who will start the bidding? One hundred dollars? Two hundred dollars?" Another voice shouted angrily. "We didn't come to see this painting. We came to see the Van Goghs, the Rembrandts. Get on with the real bids!" However, the auctioneer continued. "The son! The son! Who'll take the son?" Finally, a voice came from the very back of the room. It was the longtime gardener of the man and his son. "I'll give ten dollars for the painting." The gardener was a poor man, and this was all he could afford. "We have ten dollars; who will bid twenty?" announced the auctioneer. "Give it to him for ten. Let's see the masters." "Ten dollars is the bid; won't someone bid twenty?" The crowd was becoming angry. They did not want the picture of the son. They wanted the more worthy investments for their collections. The auctioneer pounded the gavel. "Going once, twice.

Sold for ten dollars. A man sitting on the second row shouted, "Now let's get on with the collection!" The auctioneer laid down his gavel. "I'm sorry, the auction is over." "What about the paintings?" "I am sorry. When I was called to conduct this auction, I was told of a secret stipulation in the will. I was not allowed to reveal that stipulation until this time. Only the painting of the son would be auctioned. Whoever bought that painting would inherit the entire estate, including the paintings. The man who took the son gets everything!"

God gave His son 2,000 years ago to die on a cruel cross. Much like the auctioneer, His message today is "The son, the son, who'll take the son?" Because you see, whoever takes the Son gets everything.

Much like the rich young ruler in the Bible, these persons saw and wanted the value of recognizable earthly possessions. The rich young ruler at least desired "The Son," but unfortunately, he could not part with his masterpieces to receive "The Son."

Luke also gives the account of the rich young ruler, but before Luke tells that story, he speaks about the encounter Jesus had with a lawyer.

> *Just then, a lawyer stood up to test Jesus. "Teacher," he said, "what must I do to inherit eternal life?" He said to him, "What is written in the law? What do you read there?" He answered, "You shall love the Lord your God with all your heart, and with all your soul, and with all your strength, and with all your mind; and your neighbor as yourself." And he said to him, "You have given the*

right answer; do this, and you will live."
(Luke 10:25-28).

Eternity Seems a Long Time Away

At least the lawyer knew what he needed to do, but there is no confirmation that he followed through and lived his life in the way that he knew he should. The problem with Eternal Life, as we perceive it, is that for most of us, it is a long way away. Even most of those where it might be close do not want to admit this life may be about over. Because of this, and because of our misperception that seeking to do God's will is going to mean less fun in our lives, the availability of Eternal Life with God doesn't seem to have the effect that one would expect. There is an interesting quote from C. H. Spurgeon, which puts this differently. His statement is about "Sin," which can keep us away from Eternal Life with God.

"Sin would have fewer takers if its consequences occurred immediately."

We seem to need a short time between cause and effect before the effect has much control over how we live our lives. Most would agree that there is a connection between how we live our lives and where we will spend eternity. However, we either do not think about it, or else we are counting on last-minute repentance to change our final destination.

Paul shows this contrast between sin and eternal life in the 6th Chapter of Romans.

> *For the wage paid by sin is death; the gift freely given by God is eternal life in Christ Jesus our Lord* (Rom. 6:23).

The Opposite of Eternity with God is Eternity in Hell

I think that what we miss may be that the opposite of eternal life with God is not that you just disappear when you die. That is not what Paul was talking about when he said that death is the payment for sin. The opposite of spending eternity with God is dying and spending eternity in hell. In the second chapter of 1 John, we find the promise of eternal life for all.

> *And this is what he has promised us, eternal life* (1 John 2:25).

Remember what we just read in Matthew:

> *And these will go away into eternal punishment, but the righteous into eternal life* (Matt. 25:46).

The promise in 1 John may just be all too true. We all get eternity, but not everyone in the way we might first think. There is a big difference between eternal punishment and eternal life.

The 16th chapter of Luke tells a story about a wealthy man and the beggar Lazarus. The rich man's concern was with his possessions and his lifestyle. He did not even see Lazarus at his gate, seeking the scraps from his table. After both have died, the wealthy man looks up from his place in hell, and he can see Lazarus sitting beside Abraham in heaven. The rich man asks Abraham to have pity on him, but the answer is; the wealthy man had permanently established his place in eternity by how he treated Lazarus during his lifetime. In this parable, Christ tells us that the way we live our life reflects our relationship with God. He is infinitely patient with each of us, giving us our entire life to believe in Him and accept His salvation. Conversely, we are the ones that close and lock the door from the inside and seal our fate for eternity when we refuse to believe in Him.

Eternity Has Already Started

Being in the presence of God does not have to wait until we die. If we accept the promises of God and allow them to work in our lives now, we can live this life and the next, eternity, in the presence of God. We can live without fear of the present or the future, for we are promised that God wants us to live life abundantly and that He will provide whatever we need to live according to His plan. For as the Bible tells us in 1 Corinthians:

> *"No eye has seen, no ear has heard, no mind has conceived what God has prepa*red for those who love him" (1 Cor. 2:9b, NIV).

We have a choice because of the free will that God has given us. Either we can live this life and the next in unimaginable wonder in the presence of God, as described in the scripture above, or we can live this life and the next apart from God, spending our time now and forever in eternal punishment. Considering this contrast, how can we not seek to know and do God's will in our lives? Why would we not want to claim all of His promises and be everything that God wants us to be? The only reasonable way is to live the life that God has planned for us. A life beyond our wildest imagination spending now and the rest of eternity with God. **Believe God Loves You!**

Discussion:

1. What does eternal life mean to you? _____

   _____

2. Do you believe in hell? Explain._____

   _____

   _____

3. Do you believe in Eternal Life? Explain. _____

   _____

   _____

4. Which of God's promises has meant the most in your
   life? _____

   _____

Call to Action:

1. If you have not made your choice to seek to know and do God's will in your life, do it today. If you have already made that choice, renew the decision today.

2. Record in your journal about when you made the choice to do God's will. Also, record how it has changed your life or how you expect it will change your life.

3. Claim all of His promises, and be everything that God wants you to be.

4. Live the life that God has planned for you, a life that is beyond your wildest imagination.

5. Spend now and the rest of eternity with God.

6. Live your life as if you really –

Believe God Loves You!

Appendix A, Additional Information

Baptism

The following information regarding baptism and its history before John the Baptist is presented to answer a question brought up when this material was first used in a small study group lead by the author.

For Christians, baptism is defined as the immersion or dipping of a believer in water. That symbolizes the complete renewal in the believer's life and testifies to the death, burial, and resurrection of Jesus Christ as the way of salvation. However, John the Baptist was not the first person to perform baptisms. The concept of immersing or submerging a person in water as a cleansing or purifying act was also present in the Old Testament. Some references that you may want to examine are Psalm 51:2-12 and 2 Kings 5:1-14. In addition, the radical Qumran sect which produced the Dead Sea Scrolls attempted to cleanse Judaism using purifying rites, which generally involved immersion. Along with immersion, the Essences' at Qumran emphasized repentance and submission to God's will.

John's baptism was for repentant sinners and prepared them to receive Jesus' baptism of the Holy Spirit. Jesus did not perform water baptism. Instead, his disciples performed any baptisms by water. (Reference, John 4:1-2).

Appendix B, Evaluation Form

Please copy and either mail to Marlin L Clark, 75 Holmes Pl, Tustin CA 92782, FAX to (714) 258-8443, or email to Marlin@MarlinLClark.com. An electronic copy is available on our website, http://www.MarlinLClark.com. All information provided will be for our use only. The readers of this book are our best critics., We appreciate your comments and suggestions about all aspects of the book. We would also like to know about your experiences using this book in a group study environment.

STUDY EVALUATION

Please take a moment to provide this information to help us improve the study. Many thanks for your help.

Overall Rating

Hated it   OK   Loved it

1   2   3   4   5   6   7   8   9   10

What I liked best about this study:

_____

_____

Which chapter helped you the most?

_____

_____

My suggestions for improvements:

_____

_____

What I think you should add to the study materials

_____

_____

Other comments (use the other side of the page if necessary)

_____

_____

Optional:

Name _____

Phone number _____

E-mail address (for our use only) _____

Would you like to discuss your comments?   Y   N

Are you interested in future books or studies?   Y   N

Appendix C, About the Author

Believe is the result of my search to claim God's promises for myself and to find God's plan for my life. So that you may follow some of my searchings and understand how I came to the point of writing this, I need to start by telling you some of the influences on my life.

The first influence on my life was my father. My father was my ideal. I was obsessed with being just like him in every way. He had a robust set of morals and the discipline to do what he felt was right regardless of influences that may have encouraged a different action. He did not profess a belief in God but frequently talked about "mother nature" when referring to things beyond his control relative to farming. He seemed to be in control of almost everything in his life except for the weather, which he attributed to "mother nature," but even then, he was in control of how the weather affected him.

Because of my father's influence, I decided to be an engineer at a very early age. He was not formally trained as an engineer, but he just naturally thought like an engineer and trained me in that same thought process.

One of the next influences was a Sunday school teacher that I had in the fifth or sixth grade. Recognizing her influence is somewhat strange since the only thing that I remember from that class is announcing that when I grew up, I was going to be an engineer, and one of the things that I intended to accomplish was to prove that none of the miracles in the Bible were true. If

I shocked her, she did not show it, and somehow she managed to keep my attention as we studied about God. As I have realized much later in life, God was working through her to prepare me even though, at the time, I thought that I was in her class to find out just what it was I wanted to prove was not valid.

In reality, my mother's influence was stronger than my father's. I just did not recognize that until much later in life. I am sure that she is why my sister and I went to Sunday school, and my love of speaking and telling stories is a direct inheritance from my mother.

My wife has been the most lasting influence on my life. We have been married for sixty-nine years, which is the major portion of our lives. That is hardly a record in our family, her parents were married for sixty-eight years, and my parents were married for over seventy-eight years. My wife is the reason we went to church and the only influence as an adult that occasionally brought me out of the world of engineering to acknowledge the people around me.

After our children were born and we moved to California, another Sunday school teacher influenced my life. Our senior pastor's wife taught our "Young Marrieds" adult Sunday school class for several years. She was a very spiritual person and also a very practical person. This combination, plus being a caring person who worked diligently and successfully at living a Christian life, influenced me more than I realized at the time. She was undoubtedly one of the people God used to help me understand my need for Him.

At the same time I was attempting to start a new business, an associate pastor at our church in Santa Ana, CA, started a men's prayer breakfast group. That was a fortunate coincidence (God seems to arrange many of these in my life) as I was certainly in need of support and was as open as I had ever been up to that point to letting God into my life. That was the first time I had openly admitted I needed God either to myself or to others.

In addition to people, several situations have affected my understanding of myself and my need to have God in my life.

My job with a small Systems Engineering Firm from 1964 through 1969 was the beginning of my understanding that rather than being terrified about being in front of a group of people, I actually enjoyed it. That was also where I first discovered that I had some reasonable talent for communicating ideas in the written word. Initially, these were technical reports and presentations at work, but, bit by bit, these experiences gave me the confidence to seek opportunities to lead groups in the church, teach Sunday school classes, and eventually preach.

Going out on my own for the second time was a definite growing experience. As always, one of my biggest hurdles in allowing God to work effectively in my life was my desire to "be in control." Over the twenty years of running my own company, I eventually realized that I had to accept that I was not in control—and that only by letting God take control would my life be anything like what He wanted for me.

Preaching is and has been the most significant experience in my Christian life. I feel closer to God and closer to finding His solutions to my problems while preparing for a sermon than at any other time. I think preaching is one of the ways that God wants me to witness. It is particularly gratifying when a person listening tells you that God has touched their heart through words that God has inspired you to speak.

For me, teaching is the next best thing to preaching. The preparation for a class is a time of great learning. The challenges in presenting ideas and stimulating others to develop their understanding of a subject are gratifying. In addition, the personal questions that a student may ask the teacher can be very illuminating.

ABOUT THE AUTHOR

About twenty-five years ago, we started a small group at our church that I agreed to lead. Four couples meet almost every Tuesday night at our house. We began as a series of studies on a different topic each week. I would pick the topic and select one or more biblical references relative to that topic. Two things soon happened: We became a close, cohesive, and spiritually supportive group, and we gravitated towards mostly being a Bible study group with periodic interludes on a unique book. That proved to be an ongoing point of spiritual growth in my life. Preparing lessons for this group and putting my ideas together for the sermons that I preached were the primary reason I set out to write this book about God's promises in the New Testament.

Several years ago, I discovered the books of both Catherine and Peter Marshall. While scanning through the "spiritual books section" in a discount bookstore, I came across the book "Something More" by Catherine Marshall. I knew very little of Catherine Marshall, but the name Peter Marshall rang a bell. I have grown to appreciate the struggles and triumphs in Catherine Marshall's life, and her spiritual journey, as related in her books, has greatly inspired me. I pray that those who read this book on the promises of God may gain some additional insight into their spiritual journey.

On April 10, 2006, my father, at the age of ninety-nine, journeyed in Spirit. I spent eight nights with my father after surgery to repair a broken hip, including the night he died. As explained in the chapter on prayer, these eight days have profoundly influenced my life, my relationship with God, and my understanding of at least a part of what God wants me to do with my life. Those eight days confirmed to me that there were things that God has done in my life and problems that I have had in my life that He wanted me to share with others. This book is another one of the ways that I am following His direction.